How the Brain Thinks

HOW THE BRAIN THINKS

Dr Graham J Desborough

Published by FACE MAP Ltd

Contact author: drgrahamdesborough.com

ISBN (Paperback): 978-0-473-46708-1
ISBN (EPUB): 978-0-473-46709-8

A catalogue record for this book is available from the National Library of New Zealand.

To my mum and dad

Contents

Preface

I started work on this book in the mid-1990s having researched my master's thesis about the different approaches taken in the cognitive research on Judgement and Decision-Making (JDM). I considered that what I had learned was so useful, I decided to turn my thesis into a book. I set off into the sunset, wondering if I could be the next Bertrand Russell of psychology and write the definitive book on thinking about thinking.

Yeah, right. That was twenty years ago.

The neuroscience has exploded since then, and we can now explain how the mind within the brain does things. But why do we do the things we do? How is behaviour produced? I had read one of Daniel Kahneman's books *Thinking, fast and slow,* which contains great insights into behaviour and bias, but it didn't answer the central question for me — **How does the brain think?** I feel the same lack of a central coherence in that large tome *Principles of Neural Science* fifth edition, edited by Eric Kandel and others, which I have referred to extensively in this book. There, the same words used by different authors, in the same context, have different meanings. It made me so confused, and I still could not answer the question — **How does the brain think?**

I was brought up in a house that my mum and dad built, on isolated land surrounded by regenerating native New Zealand bush which I had free access to. I was left to my own devices as there were few children of my own age around, and my parents were always busy. This meant I had plenty of spare time to happily explore the acres of uninhabited bush around the periphery of the section and to listen to the languages of birdsong. I guess I grew up to be an instinctive natural biologist. I get the interconnected hierarchy of life with its cycles of birth and death. I get biology because I can see it and relate to it without needing the lens of mathematics, and I do love browsing thick tomes such as Kandel's because, for me, they spring to life.

Luxuriating in the shower one morning, I had the last of several epiphanies, and this book in its final form came into being. I had too long been sidetracked by important functions such as language. Language is a symbolic representation of the world around us. It is an amazing tool — not unique to humans, important in communication — but not absolutely fundamental to how we think. I realised that the essential components needed for thinking could be whittled down to the faculties of attention and consciousness, emotion, memory and perception. The complexities of language in our modern world, vocal and subvocal rehearsal, its involvement in rumination and our internal narrative — and maybe even consciousness itself — is a topic in its own right and demands another book.

The final key for this book was the frontal cortex. There needed to be some co-ordinating structure or system that links these processes together. Something had to be at the centre of things, to be a planner and an overseer, and the capabilities of the frontal cortex suit that role. This was my final water-born epiphany, my own *Eureka!* moment.

I now had a concept, a basic framework, a science-based explanation which was simple and logical, coherent and consistent, and showed how neural function can produce thought and behaviour. I can use it to understand why I behave like I do, and why others behave like they do. And importantly to me, I can use it to explain the puzzles revealed to me by psychology. It has been such a useful tool. This concept has become the basis for my book.

The word *thinking* has classically been applied to contemplation, that inner analysis of our external world. In this book the word thinking has been used as a generic term to include all aspects of brain function relating to cognition when we are awake and aware.

Introduction

We have long thought of ourselves and our behaviours as irrational, unpredictable and inexplicable. But actually, we are easily and completely understandable. Our apparent irrationality and unpredictability can be explained by understanding how the mind within our brain works. Encased in its hard skull, the 1.5 kilograms of soft, jelly-like tissue of our brain can fit into the palm of our hand, and is like no other supercomputer on earth. It is both our biggest asset and, as we shall see, our biggest curse. We can now explain how the processes within the brain produce thinking and behaviour.

This remarkable organ has over 100,000 kilometres of neurons and trillions of connections between them that mirror the networked, hierarchical universe from which it has sprung. It contains around 100 different types of nerve fibres that can send signals at 100 metres per second to every corner of our bodies, and analyse the equivalent of millions of bytes of sensory information coming in every second.

The brain has two basic roles:

- To respond to our external environment as we go about our day trying to achieve our goals and satisfy that interminable internal narrative, that voice within. It produces consciousness and a defined sense of purpose, modifying information to produce a percept of the world, and acting quickly on what it feels it needs to. To do this it uses the frontal cortex and the tools of attention, consciousness, emotion, memory and perception. This is the main focus of the book.
- To support the processes, called homeostasis, that keep us alive — such as maintaining a stable internal temperature, blood pressure and blood glucose and electrolyte concentration.

I have written the book in two parts:

- The first deals with what I have called the **FACE MaP** concept, discussing its components in detail.
- The second describes the biology of the brain, including basic neuronal function, and the structures and functions of various important areas within the brain. This part includes a list of definitions of terms used in the book.

The main theme is that the components of brain function described by FACE MaP can interact with time and context to produce thinking. (This interaction will be described in much more detail in a later book.) The main aim here is to see how the massive connectome within the brain works and how it could produce the variation in human behaviour that we see every day.

Brain function has layers and layers of complexity, some of

which are deliberately mentioned in detail to show they can be accessible. But they are far from comprehensive, and hopefully they can act as an incentive for you to explore further. There are plenty of online diagrams of brain anatomy.

We all have different fingerprints, and our brains too are all programmed in subtly different ways. This book is about understanding that difference. It is an introduction only, a beginner's guide to our complex inner galaxy. It establishes FACE MaP as a simplified, robust concept for understanding brain function and how thinking happens. We can use this concept to have a deeper understanding of our own and others' behaviour.

So, welcome to FACE MaP and the ever-changing world of brain stuff. It is truly fascinating.

PART I

FACE MaP

1

The FACE MaP Concept

What is the true nature of reality? We still don't know. We may be holographic projections of our own event horizon, or simulations within a virtual realm. But we can now produce models within our own reality that can clarify some of the great philosophical questions such as: What is consciousness? or Where is the home of the soul? or Where is the mind?

The 'neuron doctrine' says the fundamental cellular unit of the brain is the neuron, just like the osteophyte is a fundamental cellular unit of bone. Armed with knowledge about neuronal function and the massive connectivity available, we can now argue that consciousness is derived from neural activity carried out by the brain. We can also argue that the soul is that part of us — part DNA, part circumstance, part memory, part emotion — which is produced by neural activity occurring within the brain. There is now good evidence that the brain is also the seat of our mind, the origin of our thoughts and behaviours, and is what we use when we think and decide and act.

In his 2011 book *The Brain is Wider Than the Sky — Why Simple Solutions Don't work in a complex world,* Bryan Appleyard suggests that 'cracking the neural code is a very distant prospect'. But neuroscience research has continued to grow exponentially since it exploded in the mid-1990s. Recently developed methods include several new imaging techniques, such as PET and functional MRI (fMRI), microelectrodes, computer analysis of brainwave activity obtained from electroencephalograph (EEG) tracings, and of course that ancient storage mechanism genetics, particularly relevant in memory.

These are all able to give us new insights into what happens in the brain when we are thinking. Now we can peer into that impenetrable black box and 'see' the brain at work. And because vision dominates perception in most of us, 'to see is to believe', with 'every picture worth a thousand words'.

So, what if there is no 'neural code'?

What if neural function does produce mind from matter?

What if the border between the 'immateriality' of thoughts and the 'material' world is, simply, the skull?

This is not a classical reductionist point of view. Perhaps incentivised by the silos that exist within academia — where words such as conscious and unconscious, affect and emotion, can be used so differently by so many different people as we shall see — we may have overcomplicated the issues. We may have overthought how we think.

We have romanticised brain function for a long time. Words like 'soul' seem to suggest an otherworldly function for our brains and minds, separate from our body and connecting with the great unknown in our universe — perhaps even with God himself, in a mystical, ethereal way. No wonder it seems less exciting and not very imaginative and appealing — a bit like life without sex, art, sport or religion — to imagine brain function as arising from the emergent properties of complex biological systems, intricately connected with our body, where a few fundamental properties can cascade together to produce something much greater than a sum of the parts.

Simplicity of function and massive connectivity that is plastic can produce complexity of action. These properties are also present in the brains of other animals and have been around for a very long time. Humans are not unique in this world. We are not alone in our abilities, and most of our biological functions are shared with other species. Over ninety per cent of our genome is present in lizard DNA, and bees can learn, and birds can speak, and mice can use emotion.

Just because we now have adequate working models of brain function doesn't mean the magic of being human evaporates. If only we could get over ourselves, not take everything so personally, look at what's around us and rejoice in the diversity of sounds, shapes, light, colour and opinion. To laugh at a joke, you don't have to know where speech, laughter and thinking come from. To enjoy music, you don't have to learn an instrument. To enjoy driving, you don't have to know how a car works.

We can still look at the stars in wonder without knowing the intricacies of astrophysics and the Big Bang — fascinating though they are — or the intricacies of how our emotions are produced by these moments. We can still read Greek mythology and feel the magic of myth and story in the same way that we can enjoy fairy tales of little green leprechauns or stories about

St Nicholas or Alice in Wonderland. We can still write wonderfully about human relationships without knowing or caring how brain and endocrine function has made those relationships develop. You don't have to be a priest or a believer to have a relationship with God.

And there is still a lot to learn. Ideas relating to connectivity and brain function are changing. Gone are the old ideas — if they ever did exist — such as static, fixed connections between neurons that fire up occasionally, like electrical wiring in your home. Now we can see that one neuron can influence many others, helping to co-ordinate firing of whole neuronal assemblies. The system exhibits plasticity, enabling the strength of signals to change with repetition (Szegedi et al., 2016). We can now see that neurons in the hippocampus can excite neurons in distant regions for several hours, a phenomenon called long-term potentiation (LTP) (Underwood, 2016). Neural connections may come out of disorganised networks instead of evolving in an ordered way (Rajan et al., 2016).

Also, neural networks don't have to rely on direct neuron-to-neuron connectivity. The cerebrospinal fluid (CSF) circulates around the brain and the spinal cord. Chemicals released into the CSF by glial cells in the brain can influence distant cells in the dorsal horn of the spinal cord. Endorphins released into the periaqueductal grey matter in the brain stem can influence signals travelling in the lateral spinothalamic tracts, influencing pain perception. Nothing in the neuroscience of the brain, it now seems, is fixed or unchangeable. In a metaphor for our age, both the science and the function of the brain are plastic.

Since the 1950s, cognitive science has led the way in research on behaviour. It has been a useful signpost, using the computer both as a tool and a model. In cognitive science the brain is largely treated as a black box, hinted at but always unexplored, unknown. Now we can explain why we behave like cognitive psychologists say we do, by using findings from neuroscience. But this doesn't render psychology or any other social science obsolete. These sciences are looking at brain function and behaviour in different ways, all adding to the total picture, and there is still a lot we don't know.

The central role of the frontal lobe

The central concept of this book is that the frontal lobe and its complex covering cortex is heavily involved with four major components of brain function:

- Attention (similar to awareness and perhaps a subset of consciousness)
- Emotion
- Memory
- Perception

The FACE MaP acronym is produced by combining these elements:

Frontal cortex
Attention
Consciousness
Emotion
Memory
and
Perception

Figure 1 shows a basic model, or schema, of thinking. It is not a diagram showing precise network connections. It is hopefully not too simplistic and has been developed as a tool to show the interrelationships between the different aspects of brain function that are essential in thinking and deciding. These aspects could also be called abilities, activities, components, elements, facilities, faculties or functions, terms that are used interchangeably in this book.

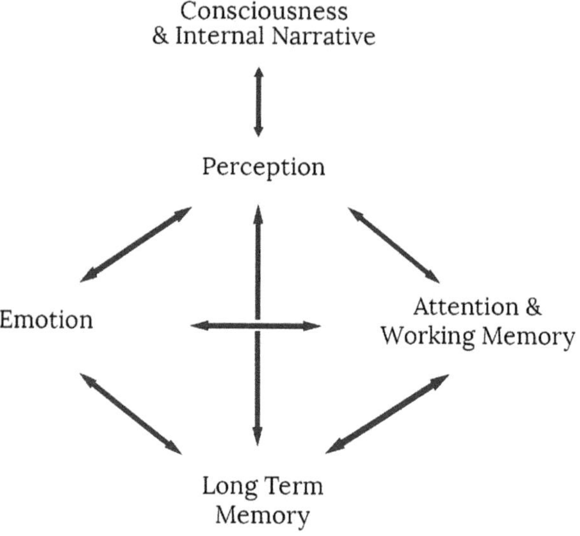

Figure 1. How thinking happens

In this model, mid-level activities within the frontal cortex, such as attention, interact with memory and emotion to produce other higher-level abilities, such as perception and consciousness and our internal narrative. These are mainly mediated by frontal cortex activity. In turn, these can influence other higher-level activities, such as thinking and deciding and acting, which lead to behaviour that can be observed.

In the following chapters we will closely examine each of the FACE MaP components. Here is a brief introduction to each of them.

Frontal Cortex

The large frontal cortex is the 'F' in FACE MaP. It is close to principal areas involved in memory, emotion and movement, and has a major role in personality and perception. It is the driver, the overseer, the executor, heavily involved with attention and working-memory and able to access long-term memory and emotion. It is wakefully prescient, suffusing consciousness with the thoughts of who we are and why we are here, where we want to go, and how to get there.

This chapter shows how this 'boss' produces the necessary control over cognition and gives us the freedom to choose how to behave. I discuss the overall structure and function and then focus on two particular areas: the ventromedial prefrontal cortex (VMPFC) and the dorsolateral prefrontal cortex (DLPFC). The VMPFC is involved in fast and slow emotional processing, and connections with the cingulate cortex enables it to also play a part in both fast and slow decision-making. The DLPFC helps carry out the closely related functions of working-memory and attention.

Attention and Consciousness

Attention is the bright light that illuminates and Consciousness is the web that holds thought together. This chapter shows how attention and consciousness, the 'A' and 'C' in FACE MaP, are produced. But does consciousness exist — or is it another human construct? Maybe consciousness is simply inwardly focused attention in a state of wakefulness that produces a heightened awareness. It could be related to perception. Maybe it is *attentionally directed perception* itself?

I also explain how a complex thought pattern such as consciousness could arise as an emergent phenomenon from a complex hierarchical system. We will analyse our internal narrative, that voice within, and our default mode network, conscious processes useful in guiding us through our day. Are *they* a large part of consciousness?

Emotion

Emotion lies at the core of our decision-making, influencing the food we buy, the partner we choose, how we drive on the motorway, how we vote and what or who we 'like' on Facebook. It underlies the success of emojis and gifs and art. Because of the way the brain has evolved, we are essentially emotional beings who also think — like, lizards with a cortex.

I attempt to answer some of the following questions: What is emotion, where does it come from and why do we feel like we feel? Emotional responses are common to many species and, just like the word 'consciousness', confusion reigns around the words emotion, feelings and affect, emotional states and mood. I discuss the varied use of these terms, then make some suggestions about how to standardise them, and introduce a new way of thinking about emotion. We find out about the subtle games of affect and reason, include some anatomy and function, and show the ways emotion is transported by story and facial reactions and why loss makes us so upset.

Memory

Memory, the 'M' in FACE MaP, is the foundation of our habits, beliefs and attitudes and can be heavily involved with emotion. Memory is always in the background, readily available, never constant, and changed by time itself and by the new experiences time brings.

Wherever we go we record events that we have paid attention to. This stored record of experience is called memory. It isn't perfect, is a semi-stable representation of all we think we know, and is really useful to us in interpreting the present appropriately. But memory is not simply one process. It reflects our complex environment and our role within it and the many ways in which we learn. Memory is plastic, malleable, changed by time and the changing circumstances time brings. It is usually divided into short-term and long-term memory.

Short-term, or working-memory, is our mind's eye, mainly produced by areas within the frontal cortex that can hold and work on information over time, using attention and emotion to produce perception. Amongst other things, it is what we use to create, problem solve, plan and execute our goals.

Long-term memory, on the other hand, is the many-roomed storehouse of our knowledge. It can be gained in many ways and recalled at different speeds. It can be classified according to whether consciousness or attention is needed for its use and what type of information it stores, such as semantic memory for words and episodic memory for experience. These latter long-term memory types are formed by acquisition and consolidation then stored, ready for recall when appropriate.

Perception

Perception is how we interpret the world around us, relying on attention to showcase, using memory to compare, and emotion to quickly say 'good' or 'bad'.

This chapter covers some of the ways in which perception has been researched, briefly touching on mathematical models that are still very much in use today. The general principles of how mechanical and chemical information is transformed into neural impulses are followed by showing how our dominant sense, vision, is produced. But vision makes mistakes, producing illusions that are constant, unlike magic that disappears when the trick is figured out. These mistakes, or biases, are important and can cause significant harm and even death if not allowed for. We will then go on to discover the effects of colour, of what art, beauty and attractiveness have in common, what music means to us, how pain hurts, the power of placebo, and how the framing of information changes our interpretation. This is so important in today's post-science, post-truth, fake-news world.

Behaviour and the processes behind behaviour can be explained by understanding how each of these components of brain activity contributes to behaviour at any one time. There is now a way to understand **How does the brain think?** Now we can understand **Why did I do this?**

Thinking cohabits with context. We don't exist in isolation. We exist within a complex environment, with a variable amount of time available to make choices, form goals, decide what to do and carry out plans. These two variables of *context* and *time* determine how the frontal cortex and the components of attention and consciousness, emotion, memory and perception interact to produce our thoughts. Context includes both our external and our internal environments.

Our **external environment** is constantly changing, and it has both physical and social components, including where we are, how this affects us and who we think we are. We are always assessing where we fit in our social hierarchy: whether we are autonomous or dependent, whether we can be assertive or whether we need to integrate (Koestler, 1967). Cultural context is part of this social context and is powerful. The musician Luke Thompson suggested that culture informs us that 'there are different ways of reacting to the same thing'. Like many things in the great melting pot of life, culture is both evocative, with the evoked emotion influencing our thoughts, and informative, showing us how to behave in context.

The largely hidden world of our **internal environment** also influences our thinking. Our habits, beliefs and attitudes about how we should act in different contexts crowd in upon us all the time. Our personality sets the tone, but hunger, pain, emotion, our background mood, drugs and sleep, amongst other things, can all affect the ways we think.

We are very goal oriented, and our goals can be divided in turn into hierarchies — goals, sub-goals and so on. A goal or sub-goal can be many things and determines how we think. If our goal is to reach a particular destination, we problem solve: we plan how to achieve it, move towards it and constantly assess our progress. Our thinking changes if our goal is to complete a simple task and changes again if we are just free thinking. As well as providing a destination, a goal or sub-goal forms a framework for deciding the relevance of the information we come across. Our conscious state includes our sense of self and our internal narrative about what the moment we are in actually means — *Why am I here?* and *What am I doing here?* — and helps to determine how we act.

And then there is **time**.

A little bit of time

Time — that elusive, invisible, swirling river that flows around us and through us, coming with us on our journey. Or so we have come to think. Time is the unbeatable, the imperceptible and the unknown. It can be unitised and measured but we have no idea what it's made of as it is so resistant to scrutiny.

Time is unseen, unrecognisable, and may be related to the continuity of space, motion and gravity. We cannot stop it, we cannot turn it back and we cannot get ahead of it. The psychological arrow of time never points backwards, condemning us to move inexorably forward. Tick. Tock. Tick. Tock. Tick. Tock.

Time itself cannot be defined. The 1979 Nobel Laureate in Physics, Steven Weinberg of the University of Texas, suggests that the function of time is to order things by preventing them from all happening at the *same* time. Take two theoretical entities called A and B. If A affects B, then B must occur later in time. Time is seen to be flowing along with us,[7] producing order in our lives.

Time could also be an illusory emergent phenomenon from the complex system that is our universe, whatever that may be. Time is a human concept, but it may not exist because we cannot determine what it is made of. We can measure time with some accuracy, but it is not an object we can see, smell, touch or taste. When we look at the horizon from a cliff, we can't see 'time' in the frame. For us, it just *is*. There is only one thing we can be sure of: whatever time may be, for each of us, in this reality, it ends (Webb, 2016).

Stephen Hawking suggests there are three arrows of time:

- The psychological arrow of time — being the direction in which we perceive time passing where we can remember the past but cannot remember the future
- The thermodynamic arrow of time — where complexity and entropy increases with increasing disorder
- The cosmological arrow of time — where the universe is constantly expanding, not contracting.

He argues that all three arrows point in the same direction and that the thermodynamic arrow influences the psychological arrow. His book *A Brief History of Time*, is a fascinating and easy read.

We are so constrained by time. All our biological processes depend on it. Our hearts can only beat within certain limits. It takes time for chemicals to move across membranes. It takes time for impulses to move down neurons. Time can be seen to be our enemy when we're rushing against the clock, but it can also be the great preparer, allowing us to get ready. The trick is to learn how best to use the time we think we have.

External time doesn't change. The second hand on our watch continues to go 'tick, tick, tick'. What varies to us is how much time we *think* we have: sometimes we have to think, decide and act quickly, while sometimes we *think* we have all the time in the world. Our perception of time can be influenced by our state of arousal, by the frequency of events we have to analyse, the type of stimulus we are presented with and our emotional state.

When we are wide awake, time appears to go fast; when we are sleepy, it appears to go slowly. Time appears to fly by if we are busy; if we have nothing to do, it drags. We judge sounds of the same length of time to be longer than a visual cue of the same length of time. When we're anxious, time seems to go so slowly; but when we're happy, it seems to go quickly. Time appears to move slowly for the young and rapidly for the old (Allman, 2014).

Theories of thinking

And so it is time that largely determines how we think. Since the first widely known reference — around 350 BC in *De Anima* (*On the Soul*) by Aristotle — human thought has been regarded as having two ways or systems or processes, where one system is used for rapid thinking and another is used for slow thinking. These have had various labels such as passion and reason, emotion and logic, intuition and analysis, feeling and knowing, experiential and cognitive, thinking fast and slow using system one and system two.

There have been other models. Ken Hammond from Boulder, Colorado developed the Cognitive Continuum Theory. Instead of fast or slow, this model describes a continuum of modes of enquiry and thinking, from rapid intuitive judgement to the slower scientific experiments that are the gold standard of analytical judgement (Dowie and Elstein, 1988).

We do have fast and slow systems, but the way we think and act in real time is much more nuanced like Hammond suggests. In our complex world we are often involved in doing several things at once and at varying speeds. At all times we need to maintain our alertness to danger and our ability to rapidly examine new information, and so we have a range of systems that can work in parallel at varying speeds at the same time. The slower systems work alongside the faster systems to safely get us to where we want to go, to do what we want to do.

Our most rapid responses involve reflex action that enables us to quickly react to dangerous situations, such as placing our hand on a hot stove. We react suddenly when something moves across our peripheral vision. These two different reactions are reflexive, often called innate or instinctive, and occur at a basic level in the hierarchy of the mind. They initially need minimal attention or memory. All other systems we use for interpreting our environment are associated with some form of memory.

Memory acts as a bank of experience to compare with the present and to help determine our future. We have a range of memory systems that work fast, from those of subconscious memory to those using more attention. Generally, the more attention we use, the slower the memory process.

We can also produce an interpretation, such as 'good' or 'bad', about a new object or a face or a new situation, in less than a tenth of a second using emotion. The 'gut feeling' that follows comes slightly later as the autonomic nervous system is activated.

Then if we have more time, we can use the systems involved with semantic and episodic memory to slowly figure out what letter comes next in a sequence, or to produce and analyse complex concepts in an argument. These slower systems can also be heavily involved with emotion, especially if choice is a factor.

Some structures may be utilised in both slower and faster ways of thinking. For instance, the cingulate cortex is implicated in decision-making. The anterior, or rostral, portion (ACC) is concerned with faster emotional responses, and the more posterior, or caudal, is involved in slower cognitive thinking. One thing we can be sure of is that there are a lot of interconnections between the various systems producing what has been called 'the dance of reason and affect' in decision-making (Finucane et al., 2000; Gehring and Willoughby, 2002; Slovic et al., 2004).

So how does thinking happen, and why do we actually do the things we do?

Real-time decision-making and action is complex and dynamic, with thoughts and decisions and actions being modified all the time. From the moment we wake up to the moment we go to sleep, our internal narrative, that voice within, guides us. As we move through our day, the action generated when we last made and acted on a decision propels us forward through an ever-changing environment. When we find ourselves paying attention to something, we use our emotions, our memories and our perceptual abilities to produce a 'percept', an interpretation of available information. Guided by that voice within, we then have to decide its relevance to us in context, and there are a range of methods available to us.

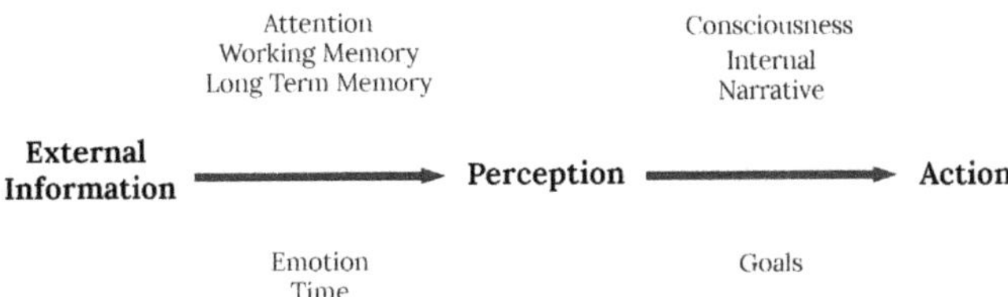

Figure 2. From information to action

But eventually, a certain threshold will be reached in the decision-moment when the need to act becomes the dominant motivator. Guided by those feelings described by cognitive science, such as optimism and overconfidence, we produce a response geared towards producing cognitive ease and resolving cognitive dissonance. All this can happen very quickly or at a more measured pace, depending on how much time we think we have.

These responses can be seen as neural activity that can be measured in a variety of ways by neuroscientists, or can be labelled as a behaviour that is seen, studied and interpreted by psychologists. The responses can be interrupted any time something catches our attention. We can be at different stages for any number of processes at the same time, but we can't use the same systems to try and perform different tasks at the same time. We can be thinking about what to cook for dinner, at the same time as talking on the phone and typing an email. But obviously we can't have two different conversations at the same time, or type two-handed and send a text at the same time, unless of course we have voice activation.

But the mind is not perfect; indeed, it may be our biggest curse, our own existential threat. In an informative interview in the back of a taxi for a BBC *Horizon* documentary on decision-making, the Nobel Laureate Daniel Kahneman was asked what he thought was our greatest weakness. 'Overconfidence' was his telling reply.

That word goes a long way to explaining why we are fearlessly rushing headlong towards the abyss. That and because vision is so central to the perception of our world for most of us. If something is out of our sight, it's out of our mind. If it's out of our mind, it's not seen as a threat. It is one reason why our oceans are so full of garbage, why we bury to forget, and why things we can't see attain an almost mystical quality.

The neural systems we use are also prone to error. For instance, the visual system that we rely on so much produces illusions that never change: the full moon rising looms large on the horizon but small at its high point; objects in the distance that are clear appear close; and objects that are blurred seem farther away. So, be careful on a misty day — that oncoming car may be closer than you think!

Cognitive psychology has informed neural science in various ways. For instance, neural models of memory recall have been produced from studies of immediate free recall (IFR) and immediate serial recall (ISR), as we shall see in the section on working-memory (Grossberg and Pearson, 2008). The relationship between psychology and neuroscience is a two-way street, a mirror of brain function itself.

One of the cornerstones of recent cognitive psychology is the study of bias, or error, where people make choices in experiments that contradict known theory. Initially these studies provided insights into how the mind works, and these insights can now be explained using a concept like FACE MaP. So, to understand FACE MaP, we now have to see how these facilities of attention and consciousness, emotion, memory and perception are produced, and how they can influence how we think and feel and act.

We will start with that important area, the frontal cortex — the F in FACE MaP, influencing everything.

2

The Frontal Cortex

The *frontal cortex* — the F in FACE MaP

A lot of what we know about brain function has come from examining the changes that occur in people with various brain lesions. These lesions could have been caused by conditions such as stroke, trauma, tumour or the complications of surgery. The functions that have been changed are then assumed to be carried out by the areas of brain that have been damaged. One of the most well-known cases is that of Phineas Gage.

Railroad construction was a risky business in America in the mid-nineteenth century. On the thirteenth of September 1868 near Cavendish, Vermont, a stocky, local-born 25-year-old railway foreman named Phineas Gage had a six-kilogram tamping rod blown through the left side of his skull in an accidental explosion. He was thrown onto his back and had brief convulsions involving his arms and legs without apparently losing consciousness.

However, he recovered quickly and was able to walk to get help, despite a horrific wound on the top of his head that spat out lumps of brain tissue when he coughed. After a successful initial debridement and closure of the wound by the local physician Dr John Martyn Harlow, who was assisted by Dr Edward Williams, Phineas had an eventful recovery. This included a later drainage of a frontal abscess by Dr Harlow. He lived for nearly twelve more years, eight of those gainfully employed as a coach driver in Chile, before eventually dying of uncontrolled epilepsy in San Francisco in May 1860.

Wikipedia (accessed December 2017) has an account of the story of Phineas Gage that is well worth reading. It gives an indication of the various theories on brain function at the time, and the difficulties faced in interpreting findings published long after the event.

Phineas had changed after the accident. Dr Harlow was also a local man and already knew Phineas. Before his accident, Phineas had been energetic and smart, able to set, plan, carry out and achieve his goals according to Dr Harlow. But on review six months after the accident, he seemed to be a different person. His thinking fluctuated; sometimes he was stubborn and persistent, at other times he suddenly changed his mind. He developed many plans but often quickly abandoned them. He was suffering from what we now call 'frontal lobe syndrome', and we can now explain why he had these symptoms.

The frontal lobe, with its associated cortex and underlying connections, has evolved to be the largest lobe of our brain. It lies in front of the central sulcus and above the lateral sulcus of the cerebral cortex. The important *prefrontal cortex* covers the front of this lobe and is involved in performing higher-order, executive-level functions in the brain.

The prefrontal cortex has three interrelated abilities that provide some of the support for these higher-order activities, including flexible, complex thinking:

- The ability to hold on to and work on information over a period of time
- Working-memory
- Prolonged and focused attention

Amongst other things, these features:

- Help us to produce our own personal narrative, rumination, our default mode network, and assists in producing and maintaining consciousness
- Allow us to produce abstract thoughts
- Enable us to plan and perform our complicated social functions, a process called executive control.

The prefrontal cortex helps to process information using either simple emotion or more complex cognition, empowering us to think both fast and slow. It is also largely responsible for our personality and intelligence.

Anatomically, the prefrontal cortex makes up thirty per cent of the total cortex and lies in the front of, or rostral to, the rest of the brain, merging with other cortical areas behind it in the frontal lobe with little clear-cut separation. There is still an ongoing debate about the precise definition of what the prefrontal cortex is and does and what separates it from other cortical areas.

Karl Brodmann was one of the first to provide a clear description of the frontal cortex. He divided the whole cerebral cortex of the brain into specific functional areas defined by the cellular structure — what he called the cytoarchitecture — and this terminology is still used today. He defined the frontal cortex in primates as having a distinctive layer of granular cells in layer VI of the cortex. He used the term 'granular cortex' to define these areas.

Using techniques such as MRI, many studies have focused on the anatomical and functional divisions within the prefrontal cortex. Broadly speaking, the prefrontal cortex can be divided into medial and lateral areas, along with areas underneath (ventral) and on top (dorsal, think dorsal fin of a shark). These areas include the dorsolateral prefrontal cortex (DLPFC), the dorsomedial prefrontal cortex (DMPFC), the ventromedial prefrontal cortex (VMPFC), and the orbitofrontal cortex (OFC).

The DLPFC corresponds to the Brodmann Areas 46, 9, 9/46, and the VMPFC to areas 11 and 14. The term orbitofrontal cortex, or orbital prefrontal cortex, describes a poorly defined area of prefrontal cortex above the bony orbit surrounding the eye. It lies between the areas of medial and lateral ventral prefrontal cortex (Carlén, 2017).

Marie Carlén is an associate professor and group leader in the Department of Neuroscience at the Karolinska Institute in Stockholm, Sweden. Her review is well worth reading for an overview of the history of, and the current difficulties in, the precise definition of prefrontal cortical areas. Her discussion about the ambiguities of definition is also relevant to many other areas of cognitive psychology and neuroscience where there is a lack of precision. The article also links to a useful brain atlas and to videos of PFC structure.

Another author and academic, Arne Dietrich, Professor of Cognitive Neuroscience at the American University of Beirut, has written extensively on the frontal cortex. He has written two books: *Introduction to Consciousness* and *How Creativity Happens in the Brain*. His 2004 article in *Psychonomic Bulletin & Review* on creativity is a very accessible read and has a good summary of the role of the frontal cortex. This article forms the basis for the next section.

Two areas of prefrontal cortex that are thought to be important in thinking and deciding and acting are the VMPFC and DLPFC. We will discuss the VMPFC first.

Lying underneath the medial side of the prefrontal cortex, the VMPFC is heavily connected with the amygdala, a nucleus in the temporal lobe that has an important role in both fast and slow emotional processing. It is also close to and well connected with the cingulate cortex that curves around and in front of the corpus callosum on the medial side of the cerebral hemispheres, and plays an active role in both fast and slow decision-making. Some authors include the anterior portion of the cingulate cortex (ACC) in their definition of the VMPFC because some features of the ACC are similar to the prefrontal cortex.

In patients with medial frontal lobe damage affecting the VMPFC, their outward behaviour appears normal and they perform well in intelligence tests. But their day-to-day functioning is affected and their social behaviour is inappropriate, showing little inhibition and a lack of moral judgement.

Thinking is done in context, and culture is an important part of that context. The values and standards that are ingrained within our cultures are a huge influence on our thinking. With its ready access to memory and emotion, the VMPFC may help us use these standards to assess the repercussions of our own behaviour and decide how to behave appropriately within the cultural context. It can also help us in our moral judgements, as our cultural beliefs define our morality.

Some patients with frontal lobe lesions and limited executive control can exhibit other unusual behaviours. Normally, when we are confronted with new information, we take a moment to process it and to think about its relevance in the context using our frontal cortex, particularly our VMPFC, to access memory and emotion. Lhermitte showed that patients with frontal lobe lesions involving the VMPFC are excessively dependent on instant cues. In these patients, just seeing an object compels them to do something with it, without the overall context being taken into account. These patients also commonly imitate inappropriate behaviours of other people.

Memory is gained from experience and acts as an information bank with which to compare current cues, to determine relevance. We can't suddenly respond to everything we come across, picking up everything we see or imitating everyone else's behaviour. It could be dangerous and very time-consuming. What if there were many objects and one of them was hot, or the behaviour we had seen was socially unacceptable? What would happen then, if we had no control?

The DLPFC lies on the lateral aspect of the prefrontal cortex. It has direct connections to the medial areas involved with emotion and affective behaviour, including the VMPFC. Functioning near the top of the hierarchy of mind, it has no direct sensory input. Instead, it uses information that has already been heavily modified, one of its main inputs coming from a widely distributed network involving the rest of the cortex. Its main output is to the premotor cortex lying right behind the DLPFC in the frontal lobe.

The DLPFC is heavily involved in the three major higher-order cognitive functions mentioned earlier: the ability to hold on to and work on information over a period of time, working-memory, and prolonged and focused attention. All three are interrelated.

- ***The ability to hold on to and work on information over a period of time:*** This is an important ability of the prefrontal cortex. It takes time to do things. The behaviour of Phineas after his accident showed that patients with frontal lobe lesions are unable to carry out tasks that need implementing bit by bit over a long period of time. Tasking and goal-related activity requires an ability to plan, to form strategies, carry them out and then finish them — activities like science experiments or creating art. It takes time and continuity of thought to experiment and create.
- ***Working-memory:*** The systems of working-memory monitor what's going on in our environment. It is a short-term, low-capacity memory that keeps information that is relevant to the situation in the front of our mind so it can be worked on. It is able to sustain continuous real-time processing depending on the amount of attention available,

and seems to be necessary for flexible, abstract and creative thinking and the strategic planning required in carrying out tasks and goals. It also provides access to long-term memory systems and is necessary for the production of consciousness, sentience, perception and our internal narrative.

- ***Attention:*** Working-memory is also directly involved with attention. The ability to maintain attention is necessary for working-memory to perform effectively, and this seems to be a function of the DLPFC in particular. Like working-memory, attention has a limited capacity that restricts both the quantity of information that can be held and the time it can be held for. This has an impact on the amount of higher-order real-time executive processing that can be carried out using attention. We cannot actively think about two things at the same time. Attention also has a direct relationship to consciousness. By choosing where we focus our attention, we can choose what part of our conscious experience we are feeling at any particular time.

The right and left frontal lobes function differently. Semantic memory is of context-free things, such as words or colours. The left DLPFC helps retrieval from semantic memory. This is useful, as Broca's and Wernicke's areas which are activated when thinking about words, are in the left hemisphere close to the left DLPFC. Activity in the right DLPFC is associated more with sustained attention (Dietrich, 2004; Kandel, 2013).

Lesions to the DLPFC produce changes in the executive control of cognition, not changes in personality and emotion. One of the common deficits in people with damage to the DLPFC is that of perseveration, where they continue to use unsuccessful strategies because they are not flexible enough in their thinking. Functional imaging in situations requiring flexible thinking shows activation of the DLPFC in normal subjects, consistent with the use of working-memory. Patients with a cognitive deficit called perseveration are unable to shift between different modes of thinking and show a reduced ability to think abstractly.

The Wisconsin Card Sorting Test (WCST) is simple and is highly sensitive to damage in the DLPFC. It is used to test for perseveration. In this test, several cards from a deck of similar cards are laid on the table side by side. The subject then selects another card from the deck and has to match it with one of the cards already on the table by using one of three properties of the images on the cards: colour, number or shape. The examiner then tells the subject whether they are right or wrong in their choice, and by trial and error this feedback leads to the person being tested discovering the sorting rule the examiner is using.

After a while, the examiner secretly changes the sorting rule and the subject needs to adapt to the new rule to make correct choices. Even when there is an obvious contradiction, those with DLPFC damage continue to use the old rule to sort the cards because their working-memory has failed (Dietrich, 2004).

To **summarise** then, we need some way of analysing information over time and accessing experience through memory. This is what the prefrontal cortex does. It produces the necessary control over cognition, helping us to make appropriate choices in context and move towards completion of our tasks and goals.

Because it has no direct sensory input, it also gives us the freedom not to have to respond to everything we come in contact with. It gives us the freedom to choose how to behave.

It has medial areas, close to the centres relating to emotion and memory that can be used in the rapid analysis of information and making moral choices. The lateral areas are heavily involved in working-memory and planning, and are close to the areas involved with movement and speech production. This allows us efficient execution of planned activity, producing the behaviours that are observed. Co-ordination of all these functions is facilitated by the large numbers of interconnections between areas and layers within the frontal cortex similar to other areas of the cerebral cortex.

While the exact nature of the connectivity within and to and from the frontal cortex is still being worked out, we have the general idea. It becomes easy to see how the frontal cortex is intimately involved in attention, consciousness, emotion, memory and perception, facilitating the analysis of the environment around us, the decisions we need to make, and our appropriate behaviour within context. It is both the enabler and the executor of our will.

3

Attention, Consciousness and Our Internal Narrative

We shall now turn our attention to ***attention*** itself, and that puzzle of puzzles, ***consciousness*** — **the A and C in FACE MaP**.

They are both intimately involved with the DLPFC, as we have just seen. But is the basic concept behind this alleged puzzle fundamentally flawed? Does consciousness exist — or is it a human construct, perhaps like emotion, produced by our own boundless imagination?

Is it a higher-order activity, similar to thinking and perception, relying on the subservient faculties of attention, emotion and memory? Maybe consciousness is simply focused attention in a state of wakefulness that produces a heightened awareness we describe as consciousness. It could be related to perception. Maybe it is *attentionally directed perception* itself?

There is no doubt that 'What is consciousness?' has been promoted as one of the great philosophical questions. Biologically, it could now be argued that consciousness is produced by neural activity carried out in the brain, and it could be defined as a state of focused awareness.

In 1967, Koestler wrote in *The Ghost in the Machine* about consciousness being an emergent phenomenon from an open-ended hierarchical system, where levels of activity in the mind that produce behaviour move from being simple and mechanical to being complex and mindful. He explains how simple mechanical information from light and heat and touch, for instance, is transformed into neural signals. This is then heavily modified to form an ordered, coherent, meaningful explanation from the chaos and disorder all around us by the ghost within the machine. Consciousness, perhaps. Remember, this was in the days before neuro-imaging techniques were widely available.

Complex hierarchies and emergent phenomena

Emergent phenomena are part of complex hierarchical systems. They occur over a wide range of states. A simple example is in the treatment of symptoms such as fever, when we often use medicines in combination to produce an effect that is more than a simple sum of the individual effects. We call this synergy. In the folklore of medicine, the addition of ibuprofen to paracetamol (acetaminophen) is thought to produce more relief from fever and pain than would be expected if either drug is used alone.

Can we predict the behaviour of a complex system with many interrelated components if we only know about the properties of the individual components? Reductionism in science is where the whole is reduced to its constituent parts, and the properties of each part are studied in order to understand the whole. But as Solé and Goodwin discuss, how do we define the constituent parts and 'how do we define the interactions that result in the higher-level behaviour'?

They take the simple example of hydrogen (H_2), oxygen (O_2) and water (H_2O). When hydrogen gas is burned in the presence of oxygen gas, a large amount of energy is released. Liquid water is also produced, totally unlike the well-known properties of the gases hydrogen and oxygen that make up the water. Knowing about the chemical bonding and chemical behaviour of hydrogen and oxygen is not enough though, to be able to predict the properties of water. But looking backwards, knowing how water behaves is consistent with the fact that it is made up of hydrogen and oxygen (Solé and Goodwin, 2000).

The fascinating BBC documentary *The Secret Life of Chaos* (2010), hosted by the urbane Professor Jim Al-Khalili from the University of Surrey in England, discusses how complexity can arise from a combination of very simple rules. He uses many examples in his quest to find how the simple elements of carbon, hydrogen, oxygen and calcium combine to produce who we are.

One of the examples Professor Al-Khalili uses is that of Professor Alan Turing, subject of the 2014 movie *The Imitation Game*, and of Bletchley Park fame. In 1953 he was one of the first mathematicians to describe complex biological events such as morphogenesis. This is the process in which complex multicellular organisms develop from a single cell, moving through the hierarchy from cells to organs to organisms, the properties of each layer more than a simple sum of its parts. The documentary is a useful introduction to the mathematics of chaos and complexity, and is available online.

An example of where simplicity of design can produce complexity over time can also be seen in the structural variation of trees. The complicated structure of tree branches can be described by a simple formula that states: grow for a season then branch in two. Repeat. This describes really well the complex patterns of tree branches of many tree species. Some species can branch more than once in a season and into more than two at a time, producing variability between species. The variations between individual trees in a single species relate, as in the human brain, to context: how long the branches grow before branching. This is related to environmental variables such as sun, soil, wind and rain, and human activity such as pruning or burning.

In the brain, neurons numbering in their billions connect individually in different ways to produce properties and abilities far removed from just adding up the abilities of single neurons. For instance, listening to music we like at levels over 115 dB produces a sense of thrill and heightened emotion that is not there if we listen at lower levels of intensity. We can also experience this intense feeling standing in the mosh pit in front of the speakers at live rock concerts. This extraordinary feeling may be caused by large numbers of neurons all firing rapidly at the same time, producing an emergent state of mind that is qualitatively different (Levitin, 2006).

Simplicity of function and massive connectivity utilising many different ways of connecting — such as electrical connections and chemical diffusion — could produce complexity of thought and action. Consciousness could be thought of as an emergent phenomenon of this biological system, arising from a combination of being awake and aware, using attention and memory to produce a perception we call consciousness. It could be pictured as the outer layer of a porous onion of hierarchy, as shown in Figure 3.

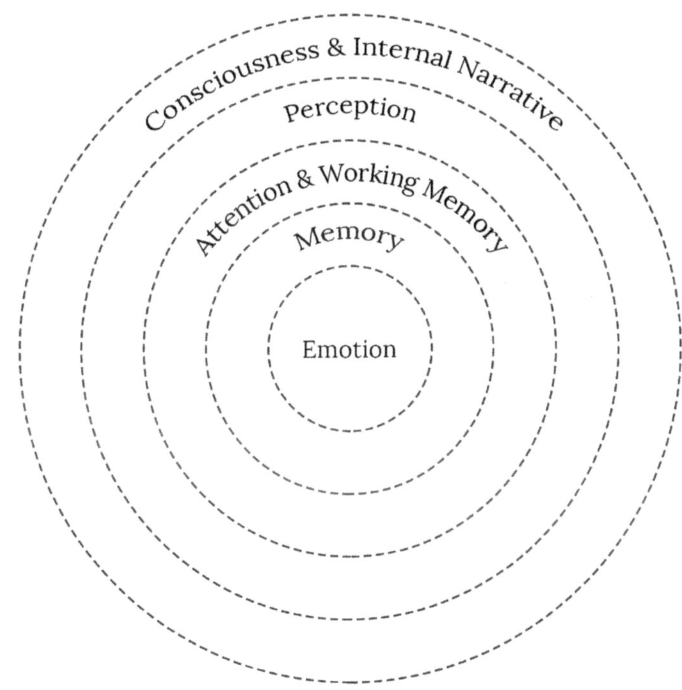

Figure 3. A hierarchy of brain function

Consciousness and our internal narrative

To neural scientists, the term 'mind' means any set of operations that is carried out within the brain. Consciousness is defined in neural science as a state of awareness. We use our consciousness when we are awake and when we dream. Sitting in the background, it is our own experience of being, producing meaning to our existence and guiding us through our day. But this subjective experience is difficult to observe. Koestler captured this well in 1967, writing that the 'self that directs the searchlight of my attention can never be caught in its focal beam'. In 2013, the American philosopher, John Searle succinctly defined consciousness as 'a unified qualitative subjectivity' that enables 'us to cope with our environment by the way of intentionality'.

Searle's apparently simple statement tells us four things about consciousness and conscious states similar to what Koestler wrote about in *The Ghost in the Machine*:

1. Consciousness enables our self, our own experience, to have a unity, a whole, a totality about it.
2. Consciousness enables us to feel the quality of our experiences.
3. Being subjective, our own conscious feelings can be felt only by ourselves and no one else.
4. Consciousness has an intentionality that helps us get where we want to go. Embedded in our consciousness is our perception of our current goal state, where we intend to go. Goal-setting works well because it provides a framework within which we can operate, our internal narrative.

Having a sense of self is also important because it produces a meaning, a state of knowing who we are and where we fit in. One of the ways we produce this sense of self is by forming a broad narrative, a storyline that seems to fit with what we know about ourselves and the world around us, and what our goals are. This broad sense of being and of place and of intention can be utilised quickly to interpret what is occupying our attention. It can be used as a framework to explain the present and predict our future.

This internal narrative that enlightens the content of our conscious experience explains why storytelling is effective at conveying information — at informing. Throughout human history, storytelling has existed across cultures, telling us and connecting with us by using examples from the past we can relate to. It can be a powerful tool for influencing knowledge, skills, beliefs and attitudes, and emotions. It can even change behaviour (Correa, 2015).

For us to listen, we need stories that are simple and real, and show how talent and intention, and sometimes stupidity, enable us to succeed. We have to be able to relate to them. They become relevant when they show events that actually happened, not those that didn't. They need to provide a coherent account that can dovetail with emotion and is consistent with what we know. However, they can be prone to error. Most stories about success do not attribute any of the success to luck, but most great success, unfortunately, is borne of luck (Kahneman, 2011).

In their 2017 article 'Chasing the rainbow: the non-conscious nature of being', David Oakley and Peter Halligan, from UCL in London and Cardiff University in Wales, suggest it is our personal narrative, not consciousness, that is important. In their view, conscious experience consists of both the 'content' of consciousness and the 'experience' of consciousness. This 'experience' of consciousness could also be called 'personal awareness' and appears similar to the 'unified qualitative subjectivity' of John Searle.

They suggest that the experience of consciousness does not control the content of consciousness; that the content of consciousness arises from 'non-conscious' executive systems within the brain that produce a continuously updated personal narrative that is not influenced by conscious mental processes. These 'non-conscious' executive systems are thought to be involved with the processing of sensory information and production of controlled behaviour. This 'non-conscious personal narrative' can be used to provide 'information for storage in autobiographical memory and is underpinned by constructs of self and agency' that also arise in 'non-conscious' systems.

Their use of the term 'non-conscious' is interesting and will be discussed in the next part of this chapter on definitions.

Zhu and his colleagues discuss major depressive disorder and its relation to the activation of what is called the 'default mode network'. The default mode network is a neural network involved in internal monitoring. It includes the processing of information about time and space that is relevant to producing our perception of self, general memory processes and autobiographical memory retrieval. This is similar to the internal narrative produced by the content of consciousness, as proposed by David Oakley and Peter Halligan in 2017.

This default mode network is a series of linked brain regions that spring into action when we are idle or distracted. It is the source of our inner monologue and the 'voice that ruminates' on our past (Martynoga, 2018). Excess rumination is where we think too much about things. It is often negative and can lead to clinical depression. Activation of the default mode network involves the medial PFC, and probably the DLPFC as well, the posterior cingulate cortex and the inferior, medial and lateral parietal cortex (Zhu et al., 2017).

In medicine, varying levels of consciousness are defined by degrees of alertness and ability to respond, and can be seen in conditions such as kidney or heart failure, blood loss, abnormal blood sugar or electrolyte levels, brain tumour or stroke. In accident and emergency departments and football pitches across the world, levels of consciousness are checked by examining how a patient responds to stimuli using tests like the Glasgow Coma Scale (GCS). This assesses three types of response in a patient — ability to open the eyes, verbal responses and motor responses.

When testing the ability of a patient to open their eyes, the examiner uses phrases such as 'Can you open your eyes for me?' and then scores according to the response — 4 for spontaneous opening, 3 for opening only on speech command, 2 for opening only on response to a painful stimulus, and 1 for not opening at all.

Similarly, when testing for verbal responses, the examiner uses phrases like 'Where are you?' or 'What day of the week is it?' Fully oriented would give a score of 5, confusion would score 4, inappropriate words 3, incomprehensible sounds 2, and no response scores 1.

For testing motor responses a phrase like 'Can you lift your leg/arm?' is used. A patient fully responding to commands would score 6, and patients able to locate the site of their pain would score 5. For drowsy patients, a noxious stimulus is used (such as pinching the ear lobe or pressing hard on the sternum or underneath the clavicle). The responses through flexion withdrawal, abnormal flexion withdrawal and full extension would be scored 4, 3 and 2 respectively. Therefore, a minimal score for a patient who is still alive is 4 and the maximum is 15. (This has been taken from information in the PRIME training course manual, 2013. The PRIME (Primary Response In Medical Emergencies) programme is funded by the Ministry of Health and ACC, and administered by St John in New Zealand.)

When discussing consciousness and whether it is necessary for calculation in artificial intelligence (AI) systems, Dehaene and his colleagues suggest that both unconscious and conscious information processing happens in the brain. They define unconscious processing as C0 consciousness.

- ***C0 consciousness*** in a medical context as described above, is about assessing concepts such as vigilance and wakefulness that are also important in discussions around sleep, coma and anaesthesia. A large amount of information processing that happens when we are awake involves C0 consciousness or non-conscious processing, such as speech and face recognition, evaluating chess-game configurations and priming.

Conscious information processing in this article is divided into C1 consciousness or 'global availability' and C2 consciousness or 'self-monitoring'.

- ***C1 consciousness or 'global availability'*** is defined here as the association between cognition and an object such as 'the driver is conscious of the light'. After our attention is drawn to an object we become conscious of that object.

Information about the object is selected for ongoing processing that may or may not involve attention and is 'globally available' by other neural systems for recall, discussion and action. It is suggested that only the information that is 'globally available' for cognition makes up C1 consciousness.

- ***C2 consciousness or 'self-monitoring'*** is where the systems involved with cognition have the ability to access, supervise and modify how information is processed. We have access to information about ourselves, such as our current body position, what we know about a range of topics and whether we may have just made a mistake. This higher-order level of consciousness that has the ability to access and modify internal representations has been called self-monitoring, introspection or 'metacognition'. The pre-frontal cortex is heavily involved in the production of both C1 and C2 consciousness (Dehaene at al., 2017).

So in this view, in the context of discussion around AI, consciousness, even when we are awake and fully functioning, has different levels of function.

- C0 consciousness is the non-conscious mental activity that happens when we are awake.
- C1 consciousness is about interpretation of the environment by 'having the information in mind' using attention and working-memory.
- C2 consciousness is at the top of the functional hierarchy, a super 'metacognition' that uses attention to turn the spotlight inwards to monitor our own internal representations, rumination and producing our sense of knowing

> about knowing. It appears to be similar to that of John Searle's definition of consciousness as a 'unified, qualitative subjectivity'.

There are others with fundamentally different points of view on consciousness, such as Philip Goff. He is an Associate Professor in Philosophy at the Central European University in Budapest and describes himself in the *Guardian* as 'an orthodox physicalist' and a 'neuro-fundamentalist'. In his book *Consciousness and Fundamental Reality*, he argues 'against the dominant solution to the mind–body problem — physicalism'. He does not believe that brain function can be fully explained by the neuronal doctrine using knowledge about the biology of the brain. He maintains there must be some other explanation.

According to his website http://www.philipgoffphilosophy.com, the book explores and defends 'a radical new alternative: Russellian monism'. This is defined by Tom McClelland of the University of Warwick as having two claims:

1. Science describes physical entities structurally without 'capturing their intrinsic nature'
2. This 'intrinsic nature of physical entities is integral to the explanation of phenomenal consciousness'. (http://www.philpapers.org — accessed 22 October 2018)

David Chalmers from New York University, writing on Goff's website, suggests that 'he makes a strong case for panpsychism, the thesis that consciousness exists at a fundamental level of physical reality, and extends this to a case for cosmopsychism, the thesis that the universe as a whole is conscious'.

Wow. With such varying definitions and such divergent points of view coming from many academics in many different institutions, this fascinating debate about the nature of consciousness, if it does indeed exist as a separate entity, is bound to continue for a long time. Silos indeed.

Darron Collins is president of the College of the Atlantic in Bar Harbor, Maine and agrees that siloism does indeed exist. Writing in the 'Working Life' section of *Science* in 2017, he says, to quote in full: 'Traditional academic disciplines, especially in the sciences, have a long history of being siloed. But if scientists are going to help solve complex problems together, we must be able to talk to others with very different perspectives'. Wise words.

Maybe we should view consciousness as having a hierarchy within which exist different categories of consciousness. The content and experience of personal consciousness could exist on a different level to global consciousness and the consciousness of the universe itself. We could divide consciousness into personal, global and universal consciousness, perhaps.

Or maybe the systems used in the default mode network that produce our inner rumination, such as the VMPFC and the medial temporal lobe, when combined with the systems used in working-memory and attention, such as the DLPFC, can also access and expand our personal narrative, our goal state and our own personal conscious state. There would simply be no need to look any further. The problem of what is personal consciousness solved. That would shatter the silos. But how dull and un-enriching! What would we talk about then?

Then, perhaps, we could get onto the ideas of global and universal consciousness. Or maybe these are just that: interesting ideas, produced by our own consciousness.

Definitions such as conscious, non-conscious, subconscious and unconscious and their use

This section discusses how use of the terms conscious, unconscious, non-conscious, subconscious, implicit, explicit, declarative and non-declarative could be rationalised.

As we have seen, there are widespread differences between various definitions of the words conscious and non-conscious. For a long time, much of our mental processing has been described as being unconscious, fuelling the debate about whether humans do have true freedom of choice and action. The power of priming is a good example of the so-called unconscious influencing an outcome. In the early twentieth century, Sigmund Freud used the term 'unconscious mental activity' and suggested that it has at least three components: implicit, dynamic and preconscious unconscious.

Implicit unconscious includes a non-conscious memory system called procedural memory that is formed when learning perceptual and motor skills.

Dynamic unconscious involves our conflicts, repressed thoughts and sexual and aggressive urges and is the part of the unconscious mind Freud studied the most.

The preconscious unconscious is most readily available to the conscious mind and is concerned with planning for immediate action. This is one of the characteristics of the DLPFC as discussed in the section on the frontal cortex (Kandel, 2013).

But there is a problem with the terms 'attention', 'consciousness' and 'awareness', and whether their use is 'implicit' or 'explicit'. Consciousness is defined medically as a state of being awake that has different grades of awareness. The word 'unconscious' is generally used to describe neural activity occurring when we are alive but showing minimal wakefulness. But the term 'unconscious' as used by Freud suggests a mental state of being awake but not being aware. Often in cognitive psychology, the word 'unconscious' is used to discuss the neural activity that occurs when we are awake but that we are not aware of. Oakley and Harrigan use another term, 'non-conscious', interchangeably with 'unconscious', to describe the mental activity that we are not aware of occurring when we are awake.

It has all become so confusing.

Maybe an adequate definition of consciousness to use within the fields of neuroscience, psychology and medicine is that of a state of mind when we are awake where different levels of awareness can exist.

Maybe a better word for neural activity that occurs when we are awake but of which we are unaware would be 'subconscious'. Non-conscious, as used by Oakley and Harrigan, could imply not being conscious. The term conscious could describe neural activity we are aware of and which occurs when we are awake. This seems logical and could avoid confusion.

So the word subconscious will now be used in this text to describe mental activity occurring when we are awake but that we are not aware of. It could replace the terms unconscious, implicit and non-declarative when describing neural activity that we are not aware of and that occurs when we are awake.

Awareness is a word similarly used in different ways in different contexts. But awareness could be simply the state of mind produced by using attention. Thinking, often termed 'conscious thought', is also a state of awareness, similar to activation of the default mode network, or our internal narrative, or our experience of consciousness. Here the wakeful spotlight of attention turns inwards to illuminate our mind's eye, that faulty plasma screen of the mind, accessing memories and moulding them into something new, using the bench-like abilities of working-memory produced by activity in the DLPFC.

'Declarative' and 'nondeclarative' are another two terms that can cause confusion. The word declarative is commonly used to describe conscious mental activity associated with attention. It is similar to subvocal rehearsal. Nondeclarative mental activity could be redefined as subconscious to avoid confusion. These two adjectives are often used when describing memory.

The useful words implicit and explicit can also be used. 'Implicit' is a word commonly used to depict unconscious mental activity and is also called nondeclarative and automatic. It is describing subconscious mental activity without the use of attention that occurs when we are awake. Likewise, the word 'explicit' is often used to depict conscious mental activity and is also called declarative and non-automatic. It is describing conscious mental activity using attention that occurs when we are awake.

Neural 'correlates of consciousness'

We are inching towards understanding the structure of other neural networks that may facilitate attention, awareness and consciousness. As we have seen earlier, the prefrontal cortex is heavily involved with attention and awareness. Siclari et al. investigated the different types of neural activity that happen in different dream states. Dream states have many similarities to consciousness and could be seen as versions of consciousness that happen while we are asleep. Our recollection of our dreams varies — sometimes we can recall them and sometimes we can't.

Different types of eye movements occur during different sleep states, and they can be investigated by correlating these sleep states with electrical activity in the brain. Electroencephalography (EEG) is a technique that measures the electrical activity of the brain in real time using electrodes within a cap placed on the scalp. This produces a tracing on paper showing wave-like patterns of activity that can vary in different states of awareness or sleep.

A type of sleep that occurs with rapid eye movements, REM sleep, is usually associated with dreaming. EEG recordings during REM activity show widespread *high-frequency* activity that is similar to when we are awake. But dreaming also occurs in sleep without rapid eye movements, called non-REM sleep, where the EEG usually shows widespread *low-frequency* activity.

By using high-density EEG, Siclari and his colleagues studied the differences in EEG recordings that occurred in REM and non-REM sleep, and whether dreams were reported or not. Reports of dreaming were associated with local decreases in the low-frequency activity in the posterior regions of the cortex. By monitoring this local low-frequency activity, they could predict whether or not the individual would report dreams during non-REM sleep, and they suggested that 'it may constitute a core correlate of conscious experiences in sleep'. This may translate into a neural correlate of consciousness, but it may just reflect the fact that a large component of our dreams is visual, and a large part of the occipital cortex is visual cortex (Siclari et al., 2017).

Sara Reardon reports that the claustrum is an area of the brain that has been looked at over the past decade as a potential pathway for the 'conductor of consciousness' by scientists such as Francis Crick of DNA fame and Christof Koch from Seattle, Washington. Using advanced imaging techniques to look at the thick, white myelinated fibres coming into and out of the claustrum in mice show that 'it is neural Grand Central Station'. This is a pathway that can potentially carry the huge amounts of visual and other 'correlates of consciousness' towards the frontal cortex and the DLPFC (Koch, 2014).

The spotlight of attention

Attention is an important part of consciousness; indeed, as mentioned before, it may be consciousness itself. What we currently call consciousness carries on in the background, but it is attention that grabs the headlines.

We are constantly bombarded by sensory stimuli. When we are awake, we can use attention to focus on specific objects or scenes or sounds or smells or tastes that we have become aware of, and we can exclude all the other things happening around us. We need to be conscious and awake in order to pay attention, and attention is like heightened, focused consciousness producing awareness. When we shut our eyes or turn off to the world, attention turns inward, improving our appreciation of sound, touch, taste and smell, magnifying our thoughts and producing a consciousness-like state.

Attention is always available, but it has its limits. It is associated with the systems of wakefulness and arousal arising in the brain stem, such as the locus coeruleus that uses the monoamine neurotransmitter noradrenalin. These systems project to areas of the frontal lobes such as the DLPFC, a prime candidate for the 'seat of attention'.

Attention influences the perception of the world around us. It points to the origin of phrases such as: 'to look but not see', 'I looked and for the first time in my life saw it as it really was', 'hiding in plain sight'. Attention is needed to help focus our perception of what the stimuli or packages of information or cues coming in to us really mean. Like consciousness, attention is needed to produce and maintain our own sense of self and to monitor our environment. It uses lots of energy.

Focusing our full attention on something for lengthy periods without rest is hard to maintain. It can rapidly shift within milliseconds from say, reading a book, to looking out the window; from talking to a friend, to listening to a track playing on the radio. When our attention is focused, the pupils in our eyes dilate; and the more we are paying attention, the more they dilate, showing where the phrase 'the eye opens a window into the soul' comes from. Contraction and dilation of the pupils are under the control of the sympathetic and parasympathetic nervous system and are also influenced by activity in the nucleus coeruleus.

And we can make mistakes if our attention is too focused on one part of our surroundings. We can unintentionally become 'inattentionally' blind. If we pay too much attention to a particular scene in front of us, we can miss other events within that scene that may be obvious to others and may be important.

There are some very funny videos about inattentional blindness. In one, subjects were asked to look at a group of dancers on a stage and count the number of times a particular activity was performed. At the same time, a person in a gorilla suit moved amongst the dancers. The hilarious film shows the gorilla walking through the dancers unnoticed by the majority of the audience because they were concentrating on counting as instructed. It is a great example of what has been termed 'inattentional blindness', or 'change blindness'. This has been replicated in many different situations many times. The TV series *Brain Games* has a whole episode dedicated to it, and there are many similar examples on social media.

Attention should be used wisely, and to be efficient, it needs to be allocated appropriately. For instance, when we multitask, short sharp bursts of attention focusing on the different tasks are needed, yet when we create, long bursts of concentrated attention are needed. Tasks require attention when we're starting and when we're stopping them. But when we are carrying out the task, we can use procedural memory subconsciously, particularly if the task has been rehearsed several times before.

And it takes time for attention to fully 'transition' from one task to another. Sophie Leroy discusses some of the influences on how attention transitions from one task to the next in the busy office spaces of today. If we leave one job unfinished, attention can't fully move on and allow us to be fully effective at the next one until all thinking about the first one stops. So we need to finish it and get 'cognitive closure'. We need to disengage, and being put under 'time pressure' helps.

Being put under time pressure helps us when we move on to our next task and also helps our next performance. Although this pressure may help us disengage from the first task, we should be aware that in some situations the previous one may have been left unfinished. So if you're doing something and the boss suddenly asks you to do something else, make a note of what you were doing before (Leroy, 2009).

If there are many tasks to be done in a day, we need to plan. We need to group those that need less attention and that use different neural systems working in parallel. We can talk on the phone while doing our nails, or write an email while talking to a colleague. Each of these uses small amounts of attention and neural systems that can work at the same time, because they run in parallel with each other and are largely independent of each other.

There are links between attention and mood and feelings as well. We have to be in the mood to pay attention and sometimes our mood lets our attention have a rest for a while. A feeling such as fear, however, concentrates and sharpens it. Some of us can sharpen our attention in different ways, such as by increasing the background noise. Some writers have long preferred to write in cafés because they say the background chatter increases their overall attention and they can concentrate (Taleb, 2012).

When we look at images that confuse us, like the drawings of Escher, we feel uneasy, and this draws our attention till we figure it out. This uneasiness has been called cognitive dissonance by psychologists.

Attention has a relationship with memory: 'I saw what was going on but didn't pay much attention so I can't remember anything'. We need attention to produce a percept and engram to commit words or scenes to semantic or episodic memory, and we need attention to recall these memories. Other types of memory can be used without attention. Procedural memories are usually formed using attention, but after repetition they can be used without attention.

In **summary** then, we can see that attention is a core component of many processes, working with emotion and memory to produce perception, helping us to stay safe and work towards our goal state. And we can also see that the debates around the ill-defined concept of consciousness are certain to continue for some time yet.

4

Emotion — At the Core of Thinking

Now we come to ***emotion*** — **the E in FACE MaP.**

Like consciousness, it is poorly defined, an ancient core component of brain function common to many species and central to how we think. For a long time emotion has thought to be so essential to the uniqueness of the human condition, a point of difference between us and the rest of life on earth. It is so much talked and written about. The choices we make on everything — such as art, politics, sex, religion, shopping for shoes or 'liking' on Facebook — are all influenced by emotion.

We float through life on a sea of uncertainty where emotion rules the waves; fear and anxiety are rife, and happiness is elusive and ephemeral. The God of Small Things constantly gives and constantly takes away. Just like time, the fine mist of emotion swirls around us, blanketing us and suffusing through us, changing our lives. Its constant prescience ebbs and flows with the changing contexts of the seconds, minutes, hours, days, months and years, influencing how we think.

In stressful situations the hormones cortisol and adrenalin are released to give us the energy and focus we need. Neural networks are activated that make our pupils dilate, our hearts race, increasing our attention and focusing us so we are ready to act quickly. This is the 'fright and flight' phenomenon.

When we are in a magical post-coital bliss, or listening to music we love, or just hanging out with our friends, the wonderful hormones oxytocin and endorphin make us feel connected, satisfied, at one with the world. Our eyelids close, our pupils become normal and we relax, pay less attention and slow down our thinking.

Emotion can also be used as a tool. It can be used to rapidly decide whether something is good or bad if we need to think quickly and intuitively, and it can be used to evaluate evidence and help us make choices when we are thinking slowly, more analytically, with the time to see if things fit.

But in 2015, in his informative column in the *Guardian Weekly*, Oliver Burkeman wrote: 'No one really has a damned clue what an emotion is'. If the thinking and the sensations related to emotion are taken away, then what is left? 'Somehow the emotion itself, as distinct from thoughts or sensations, has gone missing in action.' And it has still not quite been located, despite the enormous advances in knowledge of cognitive psychology and neuroscience and their various offshoots.

In his 1884 essay 'What is an emotion?', William James provided a graphic description of the behaviours associated with emotion. He said it is hard to imagine the emotion we call rage by imagining 'no flushing of the face, no dilation of the nostrils, no clenching of the teeth, no impulse to vigorous action, but in their stead limp muscles, calm breathing and a placid face? The present writer, for one, certainly cannot'.

Five words needing definition

To try and get some order into discussing the confusing concept of emotion five commonly used words need to be discussed:

- Emotion
- Feelings
- Affect
- Emotional states
- Mood

In neuroscience, ***emotion*** is simply our fast, initial response to an event, object or piece of information. It should perhaps be renamed as our emotional response. It is internal, unseen and largely unfelt. It is binary, like computer code, simply 'good' or 'bad', and is largely modulated by the amygdala. This rapid, instinctive response also includes a rapid estimation of how good or bad the information is. It becomes 'tagged' with a number, a valence (Damasio, 1994), and the valence increases with loss, and is relatively neutral for gain (Kahneman and Tversky, 1984).

Our ***feelings*** develop following on from this rapid initial emotional response. This is the ***affective response*** and is what most of us mean when we talk about 'emotions'. It is what William James is writing about. Developing feelings takes time, and comes as the hypothalamus and the autonomic systems are activated, producing those gut feelings we all know and have to live with.

The words ***emotional state*** and ***mood*** are synonymous. Mood lies in the background and generally changes slowly in different situations. It is the default system of the moment, returned to after an initial explosion of emotion and feelings, say, when we suddenly meet an old friend. Our mood, in turn, has a top-down influence on how we feel and how we act, and on our rapid emotional response to new information.

We are hardwired to think and decide quickly, intuitively, using emotion to label something not only good and bad, but *how* good and *how* bad. Parts of our ancient brain, such as the amygdala, hippocampus, thalamus and basal ganglia, lie close together around the top of the brain stem with the hypothalamus and the midbrain, and are common to many species. These nuclei are largely responsible for the feelings attached to emotion.

Other older neural circuits using monoamines such as serotonin and noradrenalin arise in nuclei of the brain stem — the raphe nuclei and the locus coeruleus — and have large projections to and from the forebrain and to the spinal cord, influencing mood. The serotonergic projections are the largest, with single neurons able to influence hundreds of target neurons. These 'signalling cascades' act to 'produce long-term changes in the response properties' of the targeted neurons (Kandel, 2013).

Our newer brain, or neocortex, could be called our thinking

brain. It envelops and maintains connections to these older structures. This shows that the subtle processes enabling us to think more complex thoughts embedded over time into existing processes related to emotion. At our core, we are emotional beings who have evolved to think, not thinking beings who just happen to be emotional. We are like lizards with a cortex.

Emotion and the amygdala — is this all there is?

The brain has two functions: to keep the body and itself alive, and to respond to what it sees as significant internal or external events. If we develop sudden chest pain, a whole series of events is unleashed to enable us to sort out whether this particular event is significant or not. If an external event attracts our attention, we need to rapidly decide whether it is a threat or not. One fast way we have to assess the situation is to use emotion. Some would say we use instinct, others would say we use intuition.

Emotion is defined in neuroscience as being a range of rapid automatic physiological responses that occur after our brain has detected a challenging situation. It is not what we initially feel. The brain then responds to this situation by changing the level of arousal and changing our attention, our processing of memory and our decision-strategy. We become more alert and more focused on the situation; our frontal cortex becomes more active and uses memory and emotion to further analyse and decide what we need to do. Other nuclei become involved almost simultaneously. For instance, the amygdala sends signals to brain areas such as the hypothalamus to produce the somatic responses we label as feelings (Kandel, 2013).

The amygdala is an almond-size area of grey matter in the temporal lobe that appears to have a central role in emotion and in the rapid assessment of information, with distinct populations of cells processing information in different ways. And it is well connected. In the front, it is connected to the medial frontal and prefrontal cortex. Lying close behind is the hippocampus, particularly the ventral hippocampus, which plays a large part in memory processes relating to both emotion and the production of emotional states. There are also direct connections to the hypothalamus and the autonomic nervous system, and to the nucleus accumbens in front of the hypothalamus, which is part of the ventral striatum dealing with pleasure and reward.

The amygdala is now seen as an essential component of the systems concerned with emotion. It is still commonly referred to as a component of the limbic system. The limbic system is a term used initially by the French neurologist Paul Broca in the late nineteenth century to describe an area of the brain — *limbus* is from the Latin meaning border — that formed a rim above the corpus callosum on the medial aspect of both hemispheres. The components of this system included the medial frontal lobe, the medial temporal cortex and the underlying amygdala, the hippocampus, the striatum and the cingulate gyrus that curves around the corpus callosum.

The limbic system was initially thought to play a major role in emotion, but it is a term that is now infrequently used in neuroscience. Nowadays, the medial frontal lobe is thought to be involved with executive function, and the medial temporal area with anticipation, whereas the hippocampus is involved in consolidation, storage and recall of memory. The cingulate gyrus is important in decision-making, co-ordinating sensory input with emotions and the emotional response to pain (Kandel, 2013).

The one area that has been consistently shown to be involved with emotion, and with fear in particular, is the amygdala. Other areas concerned with other emotions have remained elusive. The amygdala has a major role in the assessment of whether a stimulus is 'good' or 'bad', and in the production of fear and anxiety. This ability to simply predict the 'good' and the 'bad' rapidly is an important tool for survival. Whether drinking at a waterhole on the savannah or at the water cooler at work, it is useful to know quickly where and how bad the threats are.

And now the science behind emotional processing within the amygdala is beginning to be unravelled. It appears there is a remarkable plasticity of neuronal connection, and the projections from one region to another are much less defined and uniform when compared to the larger systems. With its small volume and large amount of connectivity, this nucleus is well placed to rapidly analyse incoming sensory information.

This complex circuitry is still being debated. Some studies suggest there is an important role for an area of the amygdala termed the 'basolateral amygdala complex' (BLA). This area shows 'synaptic plasticity' and has a role in the acquiring of associative memories that are produced as a response to both positive and negative stimuli (Namburi et al., 2015).

Memories are formed whenever our attention is drawn to a packet of information. The size of these packets can vary, whether it's the smaller stimulus, or the larger cue. Why we are drawn to some things and not others is an interesting question and includes whether the information has salience to us or not. Something has salience to us if we notice it. Why we notice one thing and not another in our environment depends on many things, including what's going on in our internal narrative, our context and goal state, and our memory. When we are examining a patient, cues such as their rate of breathing or colour of their skin will usually have more salience than what book they've brought to read.

Our response to a positive stimulus is associated with positive reinforcement; likewise, a negative stimulus is associated with negative reinforcement. Our response has become associated with either a reward or a punishment, and a memory is formed of this association between the stimulus and the type of reinforcement.

These associative memories can also be formed when we react to a stimulus that is associated with another stimulus, such as pairing of electric shocks with food, as with Pavlov's dogs. They learnt from repeated exposure to a single or paired stimulus by changing their behaviour and forming the memories associated with the event. They became conditioned. There is more on this in the section on memory.

There can also be an emotional effect. The more the amygdala and fear are associated with any situation that involves attention, the more the response and the memories generated become 'tagged' with emotion (Damasio, 1994).

Different populations of neurons within the BLA may encode the memories formed by these associations. Two different populations of BLA neurons 'undergo opposing synaptic changes following fear or reward conditioning'. The axons of one population project onto the nucleus accumbens near the hypothalamus. These are called NAc projectors. The axons of a second population of BLA neurons project to another area within the amygdala called the centromedial amygdala. These are called CeM projectors.

Positive reinforcement is supported by 'stimulation of the NAc projectors and inhibition of the CeM projectors'. Negative reinforcement is supported by 'stimulation of CeM projectors' within the BLA. This could create a cycle of fear response within the amygdala, magnifying the response to a negative stimulus, as in our reaction to loss (Namburi et al., 2015).

This dual activation-inhibition property is also shown in another circuit involving the BLA that could be involved in influencing anxiety-related behaviours. The ventral hippocampus (vHPC) is an area involved in the production and maintenance of memories, and there are projections from the BLA to the vHPC. Anxiety-related behaviours are increased when these BLA-vHPC circuits are activated, and decreased when the circuits are inhibited. This shows there is 'a role for BLA-vHPC synapses in bi-directionally controlling anxiety-related behaviours in an immediate, yet reversible, manner' (Felix-Ortiz et al., 2013).

Pavlovian conditioning has been used to study the relationship between the amygdala and learned fear in animals, and these findings have been confirmed in humans. Patients with damage to the amygdala fail to become fearful when a neutral stimulus — what Pavlov called the conditioned stimulus — is paired with an electric shock or loud noise, the unconditioned stimulus. These patients also fail to recognise facial expressions of fear and do not generate the usual autonomic fear responses (Kandel, 2013).

It could be argued that the only true emotion we have is fear or anxiety. It is loss that hurts; gains hardly affect us. The basic emotional response then could be seen as simply a binary phenomenon — like on/off, either/or, fearful or not, anxious or not — simply indicating the level of activity of the amygdala. These binary responses are simplicity crystallised, and they dovetail with our current use of social media — basic responses, like them/us and like/dislike, are so common in our vitriolic, very public, post-postmodern world.

There are plenty of similar phrases such as plus or minus, terror or joy, like or dislike, them and us, good or bad. Think hot and cold, me and you, black and white, fast and slow, or pleasure and displeasure (Barrett et al., 2007). They all point to an easy way to discriminate between useful or useless, harmless or harmful, rewarding or unrewarding.

This simple paradigm of decision-making, using the basic emotional response as a tool to rapidly determine danger in our environment, has served us well for a long time. It exists at a low level in the hierarchy of the mind, just above the level of reflex action, and when we are awake it is always ready to be used quickly. All the other tangled feelings we have long written about, all the other words we use to describe emotions, could be human constructs that describe the feelings that all experience generates, whether it's seeing a sunrise or just thinking about loved ones long passed. This would explain why Oliver Burkeman thought emotion had gone missing — because it was never there in the first place. It has always been a poorly defined human construct that tries to explain where feelings come from.

Feelings and affect

Feelings are our physical responses generated by an emotional response. This is what we describe when we say we are feeling hurt, sad, bad, mad. We cannot feel emotion but we 'feel' the response it generates.

One vivid description of the visceral nature of anxiety is in Jean-Paul Sartre's novel *Nausea* (1938). He describes how his character Antoine Roquentin suffered an anxiety attack in a café. Sartre describes the revulsion Antoine feels after being told by the waitress that the madam he had come to see for sex was not there: he was 'surrounded, seized by a slow, coloured whirlpool, a whirlpool of fog, of lights in the smoke'. He 'floated along, dazed by the luminous mists which were entering ... from all directions at once'. He was seized by 'the Nausea' and he 'dropped onto the bench', and 'no longer even knew where' he was. He 'saw the colours slowly spinning around' and 'wanted to vomit'. Brilliant.

We can also produce this automatic, autonomic, visceral effect to a lesser extent by simply thinking about different words. If we focus our attention and think about the word 'black' and then about the word 'white', or focus on the word 'bad' and then the word 'good', our feelings change rapidly and automatically.

When we concentrate on the word 'bad', our world shades towards black — we feel heavier and more restrained, we start frowning and scowling, our pupils dilate, we can become more attentive. We begin to sweat, our posture can change and we get that sinking feeling in the pit of our stomach.

When we concentrate on the word 'good', our world becomes

more colourful again — we feel lighter and less restrained, our eyes lighten and perhaps a tiny smile forms, our pupils shrink a little, we become less attentive, we sweat less, our posture relaxes and that sinking feeling dissipates.

These are our feelings elicited by the effects of emotion charging through our brains. This is the affective response, produced by the autonomic nervous system. The time it takes to change from feeling good to feeling bad about something, and vice versa, is around 100 milliseconds, or one-tenth of a second.

The autonomic motor system generates these visceral, or somatic, feelings associated with emotional states, and is called the 'affective response' or 'affect'. This system produces the fast heartbeat, rapid shallow breathing, sweaty palms, tense muscles, dilated pupils, the sinking-gut feeling and the need to flee that is associated with fear — the fright-and-flight reaction. The central co-ordinating area is the hypothalamus, located on top of the brain stem.

The hypothalamus is concerned with homeostasis. This is the regulation of the internal environment of the body, such as blood sugar and temperature. It acts on three major systems: the autonomic motor system, the endocrine system and a poorly defined neural system concerned with motivation (Kandel, 2013).

When thinking about the word 'bad', the amygdala influences the hypothalamus that stimulates the autonomic nervous system through the vagus nerve to the stomach, producing that gut feeling. The hypothalamus also stimulates a component of the endocrine system, the adrenal gland on top of the kidneys, to releases the stress hormones adrenalin and cortisol. Adrenalin makes the heart race and our muscles tense in readiness. Cortisol makes energy available to our muscles in case we have to flee. The hypothalamus through its connections with the locus coeruleus and the sympathetic nervous system causes our pupils to dilate and increases our attention and arousal.

Unfortunately, the word 'affect', like the words 'conscious' and 'unconscious', has many definitions. It can be used in a specific way to mean short-term or long-term feelings, or as a generic term to describe emotional states. The cognitive neuroscientist Antonio Damasio talks about the affective response as how good or how bad we feel about a stimulus, and how we use these feelings to make decisions. Here affect, or the affective response, and feelings are similar.

The psychologist Paul Ekman uses the generic term 'affective phenomena' to include basic emotions, emotional plots, the moods and 'affective personality traits such as hostility'. On one page of the textbook *Principles of Neural Science* (Kandel et al., 2013) the word affective is bracketed with the word emotional.

The term 'affect heuristic' has been coined by psychologists to describe the way we can think rapidly using affect. Using the affect heuristic, we label cues as good or bad and then act accordingly. It is a rapid way of interpreting information. In 2004, Slovic and his colleagues discussed 'the faint whisper of emotion called affect, which means the quality of goodness or badness that is experienced as a feeling state ... and demarcating a positive or a negative quality of a stimulus'.

Damasio also discusses gut feeling. He says thought is largely made of images. With learning, each image is marked by positive or negative feelings linked directly or indirectly to a body or visceral or somatic state. When an outcome image is tagged by a *positive* marker, it becomes a 'beacon of incentive'. When an outcome image is tagged by a *negative* marker, the alarm goes off. It is thought that these markers are useful in increasing the accuracy and the efficiency of decision-making.

Also, our feelings have a value or emotional valence; they are not all or nothing. We 'feel' more when we experience loss, compared with how we 'feel' when we make a gain. This is described in more detail at the end of the chapter.

Many words are used to describe the emotions we all experience as feelings. 'There are probably many more emotional words than there are emotions', says Ekman. He describes fifteen families of basic emotions: amusement, anger, contempt, contentment, disgust, embarrassment, excitement, fear, guilt, pride in achievement, relief, sadness or distress, satisfaction, sensory pleasure and shame.

These are based on a set of eleven common characteristics that include some distinctive universal signals such as: distinctive physiology; automatic appraisal; appearance in other primates; quick onset; brief duration; distinctive thoughts, memories and images; and distinctive subjective feelings. Combing the fifteen basic motions, each with eleven characteristics, shows the large number of emotional responses that can be generated. When talking about love, Ekman's view is that both romantic love and parental love involve longer emotional plots that are 'more specific, more enduring, than the basic emotions' (Ekman, 1999).

Neural correlates of feelings can be seen in subjects asked to re-experience specific states of feeling while being scanned using PET. Activity changed in the insular cortex, cingulate cortex, the secondary somatosensory cortex and the brain stem. The pattern of change was different for the feelings studied — sadness, anger, fear and happiness. Interestingly, the amygdala was not seen to be activated during these states of conscious feeling in this study, perhaps because it is mainly involved in rapid, subconscious emotional assessment.

These areas, as well as the primary somatosensory cortex, are also involved in social feelings, such as empathy for pain, and compassion and admiration. But bilateral damage to the insular cortices by herpes simplex encephalitis does not eliminate emotional feelings. Parts of the insular cortex activated during the recall of feelings are also activated during the conscious perception of pain and temperature, confirming the link between emotion and perception (Kandel et al., 2013).

Emotional states and mood

'What name can one give it? Frustration? Depression? When melancholy sets in, a kind of invisible but thick and heavy fog invades the heart, envelops the body, constricting its very core. All we feel is this constriction, this haze around us. We don't even understand at first what it is that grips us.'

That is Alexander Solzhenitsyn's description of the mood of depression in Chapter 5 of his novel *Cancer Ward.*

Emotional responses and feelings generated are generally short-term phenomena and can rapidly fade. Feelings and emotional states that exist for longer are defined as moods. Moods last longer, have different causes and are saturated with feelings. Moods exist in the background, changing slowly, largely unrelated to the current environment but influencing how we think and act. The commonest serious disorders of brain function are related to mood and anxiety. 'Mood disorders involve either depression or elation, and anxiety disorders involve abnormal regulation of the powerful emotion fear' (Kandel, 2013).

Mood disorders can be *caused* by changes in brain structure and function, and *can themselves cause* changes in brain structure and function. Phineas Gage lost a portion of his left frontal lobe due to a penetrating injury, leading to changes in his emotional responses and decision-making. PET scanning in patients with depression show reduced activity in the subungual sector of the anterior cingulate gyrus, whereas patients who are not depressed but are asked to recall a sad event show increased activity in this area. In MRI studies of patients with chronic depression, this area shows reduced volume. Similarly, areas within the hippocampus show reduced volume in patients with depression, producing the well-known memory loss associated with this common mood disorder (Kandel, 2013).

Changes in emotional processing may underlie many psychiatric disease states. When subjects who have been under stress for a prolonged time undergo relaxation training, there is a reduction in the density of neurons in the right basolateral amygdala (Hölzel, 2010).

Anxiety states are generally associated with an increase in the size of the amygdala, whereas personality types such as psychopaths, who display little emotion, tend to have a smaller amygdala.

Maybe our base emotional state is anxiety, natural enough in an uncertain world. Maybe it disappears during those few ephemeral times when we are happy, returning when things become less certain. Maybe happiness is just an absence of anxiety. The emotion we call love is a many-headed hydra, and we can feel it intensely when it is lost — that tension between wanting and having and losing, sex and pleasure, family, legacy. But what is love? Many older cultures had different words for different states of love, but today these subtleties have been largely substituted by sex. And what is happiness? Where does it exist within the pantheon, and how is it produced?

Or maybe we have been seduced by pictures of happiness that don't ring true. Again, in the prescient words of Alexander Solzhenitsyn, in Chapter 20 of *Cancer Ward*:

It is not our level of prosperity that makes for happiness but the kinship of heart to heart and the way we look at the world. Both attitudes lie within our power, so that a man is happy as long as he chooses to be happy, and no one can stop him.

It is such a relevant message today in our rapidly depleting world, and it has been echoed in neuroscience. Feelings make us happy, not 'prosperity'. Happiness can't be bought.

Emotion and mood can influence most aspects of brain function

Whatever we call them, we cannot escape from our fleeting emotions and their associated feelings, with their labels such as guilt, fear and anxiety, happiness and contentment, or our more prolonged moods. Whether time's going fast or slow, our emotions have a huge influence on how we think and act. They are the elephant in the room where thinking occurs, major influences on consciousness and attention, on the use of memory and on how we perceive our situation.

Anxiety makes us alert, increases our attention and helps select the memory we use to interpret what we have perceived. Time seems to go slowly when we are anxious or afraid and seems to speed up when the pressure's off or when we're happy (Allman et al., 2014). If we are in a good mood when we make a choice, we feel happier about the choice. If we are unhappy when we make a choice, doubt and regret set in and we make attempts to justify our choice. Happy people make happy choices. Sad people make sad choices (Slovic et al., 2004).

We can also be primed to think with emotion. Priming is where exposure to a concept can subtly influence later thinking. It is a subtle subconscious use of memory. In a study by Zhu and his colleagues in 2015, the assessment of emotional concepts changed depending on the type of stimulus they were exposed to.

Participants who had been exposed to an *emotional* stimulus were more likely to group concepts that had 'emotional associations' than those who had been exposed to a *neutral* stimulus. Participants whose mood was influenced 'were also more efficient in categorising concepts' with a 'specific emotional meaning' that was the same as their own. There are more examples of the interesting concept of priming in the section on memory.

Emotional states are adaptive — anger is useful because its surge of energy helps remove something in our way; fear helps us move quickly away from danger. And our needs are related to our emotions — an unsatisfied need produces an emotional response — and we use our emotions to help satisfy the need, to find the food to feed the hunger. Hunger produces anxiety, and we can use this anxiety in a restless search for food.

In 1943, Abraham Maslow wrote his classic paper titled 'A Theory of Human Motivation'. It is one of the more readable psychological texts and is easily accessible online. He describes humans as 'perpetually "wanting" animals', and he ranked human needs, beginning with the more basic or 'prepotent' needs. These 'monopolise the consciousness' until satisfied. When a need is fairly well satisfied, the next prepotent need emerges, and it then dominates the conscious life and serves as 'the centre of organisation of behaviour' until it too is satisfied and no longer acts as a motivator. He ranked the needs from physiological through safety, love and self-esteem to self-actualisation.

Maslow argued that the base physiological needs relate to hunger and sex. These originated from the need to exist and to obtain a secure supply of things necessary to do this, such as food and the desire to procreate. In Maslow's hierarchy, the next prepotent need is that of safety. Those lucky adults in stable societies, that are healthy and normal, are largely satisfied in their safety needs. There is no sabre-toothed tiger prowling around outside the cave, and takeaways are just around the corner. These needs are seen to be expressed by 'neurotic or near-neurotic individuals, and ... the economic and social underdogs'. For the lucky ones, 'the expressions of safety needs' can be seen in things like long-term job protection and insurance.

Other broader aspects of the attempt to seek safety and stability in the world are seen in our preference for familiar rather than unfamiliar things, or the known rather than the unknown. Think of how we stick to brands we know when we're shopping. It is interesting that Maslow thought the tendency to believe in some religion or world philosophy that organises the universe and the people in it into some sort of coherent, meaningful whole is also, in part, motivated by safety-seeking. He lists science and philosophy in general as partially motivated by safety needs. Otherwise the need for safety is seen as an 'active and dominant mobiliser' of the organism's resources only in emergencies such as war, disease, natural catastrophes, crime waves, societal disruption, neurosis and brain injury.

If both physiological and safety needs are satisfied, then Maslow thought that needs for love and affection and belongingness emerge. 'Now the person will feel keenly, as never before, the absence of friends, or a sweetheart, or a wife, or children. He will hunger for affectionate relations with people in general, namely, for a place in his group, and he will strive with great intensity to achieve this goal. He will want to attain such a place more than anything else in the world and may even forget that once, when he was hungry, he sneered at love' (Maslow, 1943). That is a really nice piece about emotion, written with feeling.

When our needs are satisfied and we are in an appropriate emotional frame, anything can happen. Kary Mullis describes the events that eventually led to his discovery of the Polymerase chain reaction (PCR). The PCR has revolutionised the study of DNA. Just as you can't make a cake with one grain of sugar, so it is with DNA. Using tiny amounts of specimen tissue, the PCR produces enough DNA to be analysed.

Travelling to his holiday home in the mountains of northern California near midnight on a quiet, moonlit Friday night in April 1983, in his warm car and with his friend asleep beside him, Mullis had his own eureka moment. In a relaxed emotional state, he allowed his mind to wander. The components of the reaction that had existed separately for fifteen years were chunked onto his working-memory bench and thought about, removed from emotion. An epiphany happened. He was in the zone. His account in *Scientific American* is well worth the read.

Greg Mortenson tells the story of Jean Hoerni, a Swiss-born physicist with a degree from Cambridge who became a multimillion-dollar IT entrepreneur in Silicon Valley, California. Apparently, while in the shower one day, he watched as the water ran in rivulets over his hands. He had been working on how to store more information in computers and as he watched the streams of water he had his own eureka moment.

Rivulets increase the surface area of water. Hoerni soon realised that silicon could be packed in similar layers on a circuit board, dramatically increasing the surface area, and therefore the capacity for storage, without dramatically increasing the volume. This is similar to the folds in the cerebral cortex. Hoerni patented the idea, and from this was born the precursor to the silicon chip. Maybe the shower produced a relaxed womb-like state where, safe and free and warm, he also was able to roam in a realm detached from emotions. Timothy Leary, like, without the acid.

And in art, attention, emotion, memory and perception all interact to make us connect with the artist. Art is a way of seeing ourselves and the world around us. It is produced by the ability and the creativity of the artist, where thoughts and ideas, laden with emotion and feeling, mishmash with technique to produce something memorable. It has a strong sensory element (visual, tactile, aural) that is attended to, perceived then judged, producing a feeling of 'like' or 'dislike'.

'Good art' has connectivity precisely because it appeals to emotion, drawing us in. A piece can have appropriate structure, form and composition but will only appeal if it somehow relates to us emotionally and grabs us by the heart strings. And the 'like' or 'dislike' is instant.

Our relationship with landscape is also emotional. Connecting with the landscape of home connects us to our past, increasing our knowledge about who we are and where we came from. It solidifies our sense of self and our internal narrative, so essential for self-esteem and the ability to relate to the world positively.

When that landscape of home changes, the emotions elicited can be very raw and powerful, particularly when we have no control over what happens. The NIMBY — not in my backyard — effect produces strong reactions, that can make it very difficult to plan the placement of windmills for wind power and dams for hydroelectricity, for instance.

As mentioned previously, emotions and memory are inextricably linked. The emotional state we are in at the time of laying down the memory is important: memories attached to emotion last longer and are more easily recalled, with the attached emotion being felt on recall. Those emotional moments with our first love amidst golden sunsets are long remembered. Recurrent depression reduces hippocampal volume and changes the function of the prefrontal cortex. This alters attention and may affect encoding of memory (Kandel, 2013).

The effect of story

The telling of story is so useful. Presenting information using story and narrative produces a bigger affective response than giving the same information as facts and figures. Warnings are more effective if subjects are told a frightening story about an event instead of just being told the frequency of the event happening. Runners judged their marathon performance more accurately when given information as a narrative than when they were given bar graphs (Slovic et al., 2004).

The telling of story is an effective way of instructing us in our beliefs and transmitting culture, history and myths, lessons in life and knowledge. They can be of hope or despair, success or failure, strength or weakness, corruption, resilience, redemption, optimism, achievement and triumph. Stories are simple aggregated sets of data, examples that show us how a particular combination of events within a particular context, can lead to a particular conclusion. We get drawn into the characters and their situation. We follow them to see how they react and to see how it all turns out, for good or bad. Because of their presentation as story, these examples are easily remembered and can be used to help us in similar situations in the future.

Understanding can often be conveyed by story more effectively than by other teaching methods, such as lecturing or rote learning. One of the reasons why this happens is that stories produce an emotional response in us, sticking in our memories and lighting the road of our future like beacons. Telling story can remind us, teach us and ground us.

But we should also remember that stories repeated often can also be used as propaganda and in these days of 'fake news' can become very powerful. Constant repetition of simple phrases and sound bites enables efficient encoding in memory, and if repeated over and over again they become internalised as truth. They are then readily available because of recency as we shall see in the section on working-memory. The 'availability heuristic', as described by Tversky and Kahneman in 1974, relies on this.

There is an idea arising from neural science, and the study of consciousness in particular, that each of us has an 'awareness of self that is the centre of experience' (Searle 2013). We can only experience this subjective awareness ourselves, no one else can. Having a sense of self is central to the way we experience our life, as it produces a state of knowing who we are and where we fit in.

One of the ways we produce this sense of self is to form a broad personal narrative, a story that seems to fit with what we know about ourselves and the world, either *non-consciously*, as discussed by Oakley and Halligan, or *consciously*, as discussed by Dehaene and colleagues. This broad sense of being and of place can be used quickly to interpret what has captured our attention and gives us a framework to predict the future.

Storytelling has existed across cultures throughout human history, connecting with us, telling us and persuading us, using examples from the past, present or future, of magic, myth and truth that we can relate to. It can be a powerful tool for influencing knowledge, skills, beliefs, attitudes and emotions. It can even change behaviour.

For this to happen, the story has to be transported across time and space and culture to make a strong connection with those receiving it. This connection is more likely to occur if we are emotionally drawn into the narrative, empathising with the characters and able to imagine the world in which the scenes are played out. This strong connection may help explain 'how changes in beliefs occur after reading or listening to a narrative' (Correa, 2015).

This transportation also depends on audience characteristics, such as their familiarity with the topic, how much attention they are paying to the narrative, and how easily transportable they are. Van Laer and colleagues also 'found that transportation can increase emotions, thoughts, beliefs, attitudes, and intentions that are consistent with those of the narrative', but unfortunately can 'also reduce critical thoughts'.

Some of the processes used during transportation are those of 'encoding into, and retrieval from, long-term memory', where visual stimuli are matched to 'long-term episodic memories' using periods of concentrated attention, and where 'visual working-memory' is activated. The prefrontal cortex again plays an important role (Correa, 2015).

For us to listen, we need stories that are simple and real and show how talent and intention, and sometimes stupidity, enable us to succeed. We have to be able to relate to them. They become more relevant when they show events that actually happened, not those that didn't. They need to provide a coherent account which we can empathise with and is consistent with what we know. However, they can be prone to error. Most stories about success do not attribute any of the success to luck; but most great success, unfortunately, is born of luck (Kahneman, 2011).

So use story wisely. There can be huge benefits if the right story is chosen for the context, but there can be a huge downside if the wrong one is chosen. Be very careful when telling your kids bad things.

Understanding facial expressions

From an early age we can recognise faces, and we store a large number of faces in our library of memory that we can use for interpretation. Our face is our mask that rapidly conveys a lot of information and is both evocative and informative. Looking at a face evokes an emotional response in us: our own face changes subtly. When an actor changes their mask, our feelings towards their character change instantly, even though it is the same person in the same clothes. This is reflected in our response. We can laugh or cry, be happy or be scared. Solzhenitsyn wrote, in 1969, that 'the shadow of pain passed across his face'. This is a good example of how facial expression can inform us of the emotional state of that person.

Recognition of face and the production of expressions are a fundamental aspect of human non-verbal communication. From a face, we can recognise a person as well as their mood and their feelings — the various faces of anger, mirth, sadness, despair, love and attraction are well known to all of us. This is very useful in rapid risk assessment — we want to know whether the person we are looking at is a danger to us, and we want to know now! It is one reason why tinted windows in vehicles are dangerous if we cannot see the face of the driver inside. It is helpful to know what a person who is driving a two-tonne machine is doing, where they are looking or whether they are distracted as they hurtle towards you. You want some clue as to their emotional state.

From the tiny changes in facial movements in response to questions called micro-expressions, we can see whether a person is lying or not. Dr Paul Ekman, briefly mentioned before in the section on affect, became well known for his work on micro-expressions while Professor of Psychology in the Department of Psychiatry at the University of California in San Francisco. In 1985, his book *Telling Lies — Clues to Deceit in the Marketplace, Politics, and Marriage* was published and formed the basis of the TV series *Lie to Me,* released in the United Kingdom in May 2009. The series starred Tim Roth as the character Dr Cal Lightman who was loosely based on Professor Ekman.

Micro-expressions are 'intense expressions of concealed emotion' and, along with other behaviours such as gesture, voice, posture, words and gaze, help form our repertoire of non-verbal communication skills. We have already seen how pupils can rapidly dilate with attention and in reaction to emotions such as fear. Micro-expressions occur rapidly, lasting around fifty microseconds. They involve tiny facial muscles, particularly around the mouth and eyes. Professor Ekman has described up to a thousand of these expressions (Henley, 2009).

In 2009, John Henley interviewed Dr Ekman for the *Guardian* on the release of *Lie to Me*. He tells that, in the late 1960s Dr Ekman was addressing a group of young psychiatrists in training. One of the problems they had was how to predict whether a patient was lying. Patients in psychiatric hospitals who have previously attempted suicide are often full-time residents who are allowed temporary weekend leave if they have made good progress and say they are feeling better. Unfortunately, some of these patients go home and commit suicide. The problem is how do you know if the patient who says they are feeling better is telling the truth? How do you know if they are lying?

Ekman had already recorded 'a series of twelve-minute interviews with patients at the hospital' when a patient disclosed that she had lied in a previous interview. So Ekman retrieved the film, sat down and played it back. At normal speed he saw nothing unusual, so he slowed the film down and looked at it again. At the slower speed he still saw nothing unusual, so he slowed it down further and looked at it once more.

Suddenly, he had his eureka moment. Across a few frames at a slower speed, he saw an 'intense expression of extreme anguish' lasting 'less than a fifteenth of a second'. He saw three more examples of these micro-expressions in the same interview when he looked again.

Over the next forty years, Ekman showed that the seven basic emotions of 'anger, disgust, contempt, fear, surprise, happiness and sadness' are expressed in ways that are 'essentially the same, regardless of language and culture, from the US to Japan, Brazil to Papua New Guinea'. Also, these 'expressions of emotion are involuntary; they are almost impossible to suppress or to conceal'. Of course, we can try. That's what successful lying is all about.

Charles Darwin had also alluded to the evocative and informative power of facial expression over one hundred years earlier.

At the London Zoo on a warm day in late March 1838, Darwin looked at the face of a female orangutan and could see by her facial expressions what she was feeling (Weiner, 2006). He later published *The Expression of the Emotions in Man and Animals*, released in 1872. He was one of the first modern authors to recognise that internal feelings can be broadcast in facial expressions. A century later, Solzhenitsyn wrote about a patient in *Cancer Ward* seeing the quick flicker of pain passing as a shadow over another patient's face.

Neural science suggests that a specialised region in the inferior temporal lobe called the fusiform gyrus, is involved in facial recognition. Here, specialised overlapping clumps or nodes of neurons each encode different features of complex stimuli, such as faces.

From the fusiform gyrus there are projections to the entorhinal cortex and the hippocampal formation that are involved with long-term memory storage and retrieval, and to areas in the prefrontal cortex involved with perception of visual categories, visual working-memory and recall of stored memories.

There are also projections to that centre of emotion, the amygdala. The amygdala is thought to apply an emotional value to sensory stimuli and to 'engage the cognitive and visceral components of emotion' through connections to the hypothalamus and the autonomic nervous system as we have seen earlier (Kandel, 2013).

There are other interesting characteristics of facial recognition. It is important to be able to rapidly recognise a familiar face, because recognition of familiarity enhances social cohesion and the swift analysis of threat. Facial recognition processes are different for familiar and non-familiar faces, enabling us to recognise familiar faces quicker under normal conditions and easier in difficult conditions, such as low light.

We recognise familiar faces based on 'internal' features, such as the eyes, nose and mouth. We can easily recognise a familiar face in different situations, such as when it is expressing a range of emotions and when it is looked at from different viewpoints, such as from the side and the back. In contrast, we recognise a face as unfamiliar by 'external' features, such as the hairline and the ears. Unfamiliar face recognition is highly prone to error under different expressions and different viewpoints (Landi and Freiwald, 2017).

Emotions around loss

There are some early studies of risky choice between two different gambles, where either a gain or a loss was the only possible outcome. These showed that when gain is certain, we are risk averse; and where a loss is certain, we are risk-takers.

This effect is illustrated in the following study done by Kahneman and Tversky in 1984. The number of participants was 150. The first set of instructions was:

Imagine you face the following pair of concurrent decisions. First, examine both decisions, then, indicate the options you prefer:

Decision 1

Choose between:

A) a sure gain of $240
B) a 25% chance of gaining $1000 and 75% chance of gaining nothing.

The result: 84% chose option A.

Decision 2

Choose between:

C) a sure loss of $750
D) a 75% chance of losing $1000 and 25% chance of losing nothing.

The result: 87% chose option D.

Thus the large majority made a risk-averse choice for the sure gain in the first problem, and a large majority made a risk-seeking choice for the sure loss in the second problem.

Loss hurts. The power of love and romance may be related to our fear of losing it. News sells because news is mainly about loss and negative experience. Our memories of negative experiences weigh heavily on our minds, whereas memories from our positive experiences float gently along, carrying little emotional weight. In psychological terms, the perceived negative value of every unit of loss is much more than the perceived value of an equivalent gain.

To demonstrate this, we can plot the numbers of gains on the positive portion of the X-axis, and the numbers of losses on the negative portion. By plotting the perceived value of those losses or gains on the Y-axis, a value function curve is obtained. The curve is described as being concave for gains and convex for losses and the slope of the curve is much steeper for losses than it is for gains.

This has led to the concept of 'loss aversion', where 'a loss of $X is more aversive than a gain of $X'. It also explains the reason that people are reluctant to bet on a fair coin for equal stakes, as the attractiveness of the gain cannot make up for the feeling of aversion we get when we lose the same amount. Most undergraduates in a particular sample 'refused to stake $10 on the toss of a coin if they stood to win less than $30' (Kahneman and Tversky, 1984).

These findings from psychology have been reinforced by findings from neuroscience. In EEG studies of the electrical activity of the brain in 2002, Gehring and Willoughby had twelve participants make choices in a two-choice 'monetary gambling task'. The subjects were then told whether they had lost or gained, and what the outcome of the other choice was. EEG recordings were used to measure where the spikes of electrical activity were produced when they were given the results.

A negative 'event-related potential' (ERP) was 'probably generated by a medial-frontal region in or near the anterior cingulate cortex (ACC)'. This occurred 'within 265 milliseconds after' participants were presented with the results. The medial frontal cortex is close to the amygdala and the anterior cingulate cortex, forming part of the system involved with the assessment of reward and loss.

The size of the spike 'was greater when a participant's choice between two alternatives resulted in a loss than when it resulted in a gain'. Gains did not produce 'the medial-frontal activity, even when the alternative choice would have yielded a greater gain, and losses elicited the activity even when the alternative choice would have yielded a greater loss'. Paradoxically, 'choices made after losses were riskier and were associated with greater loss-related activity than choices made after gains' (Gehring and Willoughby, 2002).

This skewed relationship between perception and emotional response is evident in other studies of risky choice. In the real world there is a positive relationship between risk and benefit — there can be no benefit without taking some risk. But in our inner emotional world, there is an inverse relationship between risk and benefit that is multiplied by the strength of feelings about the risky activity. This is independent of the *real* probability of the risk or benefit of that activity (Slovic et al., 2004).

When we have been told about risk, our mood and perception of it changes. We will feel good about a choice if we are told either the benefit is high or the risk is low. And if we are told the benefit is low and the risk is high, we will feel bad about that choice. Conversely, if we are feeling good when we are told about an activity, we will judge the risk to be low and the benefits to be high. If we are feeling bad when we are told about an activity, we will judge the risk high and the benefit low, no matter what the true probability is (Slovic et al., 2004).

So we can see how the mood we are in directly influences our judgement. And this has been shown in many domains, such as in our use of nuclear power, insecticides, chemicals and money. If we feel good about unfamiliar stocks in the market, we perceive the investment in these stocks as having a high benefit and a low risk. For stocks where companies have a positive brand image and feel 'familiar', high risk is associated with high perceived benefit. If the outcome of a gamble is emotionally powerful, large changes in probability from 0.01 to 0.99 have no influence on the attractiveness of the outcome (Slovic et al., 2004).

So, be careful when and what you buy. There is no substitute for careful analysis of investments, but even then it can go wrong. Probability is a key, but it's a tool that needs to be learned, bearing in mind no one can predict the future with certainty. The last half of *Nudge — Improving decisions about health, wealth, and happiness*, written by Richard Thaler and Cass Sunstein in 2008, is really helpful.

So, to **summarise** emotion in a nutshell then: It lies in the realm of our subconscious, ever prescient. It can work both fast and slow, and varies with time and context. It can be very unpredictable. It influences our feelings and our moods and shapes our thinking. We are basically emotional animals that can also think a lot.

5

Memory — Stored Experience

Now we move away from the unpredictable roller coaster that is emotion and focus on the past — how we remember it and how it can influence the present and affect our future. We will examine ***memory*** — **the M in FACE MaP**.

As we move through life, we automatically record all our experiences that we pay attention to. This record is mostly accurate, always representative, and can't be completely erased. We call this recording a memory. Without experience, we can have no memories. Like stories, memories can act as a guide to interpret the present and show us what we need to do. In creating a memory, the experience is captured or acquired, then encoded, consolidated and stored in a way that helps later retrieval (Kandel, 2013).

Learning is slightly different. It is all about changing behaviour. When we learn, we transform our experiences into knowledge we can then use to change our behaviour. Learning changes the way we do things, is based on these past experiences and creates new memories along the way as we test our new knowledge. And these new memories are different from the experiences that created them.

Memory processes are generally grouped into either a short-term memory called working-memory, or the more familiar long-term memory. Long-term memory is such a key part of our individual and collective identity. Our genes contribute towards attributes such as personality and physique, but we are born with minimal long-term memories — a blank slate, a '*tabula rasa*'. On this blank slate is etched the memories and knowledge gained from our experiences that subtly change the connectivity within our brains, making every one of us unique. It could be argued that there is no 'original sin' and it is our experiences that shape us into being 'good' or 'bad' or 'evil'.

Unfortunately, long-term memory is not like a video recording. It's like a moth-eaten patchwork quilt that degrades gracefully and unpredictably as time goes by. Long-term memory is the many-roomed storehouse of our own knowledge. Swayed by emotion, it is the foundation of our habits, beliefs and attitudes, always in the background, readily available, never constant, changed by time itself and by the new experiences time brings, giving us a repertoire to draw on when interpreting current situations.

Working-memory

Working-memory is a conscious memory system requiring active participation and using attention. It temporarily maintains and manipulates information relevant to our goals at the time. Working-memory is thought to be a low-capacity memory that is instantly available for use. It can use current information from external sources, such as smell and taste, or it can come from memory recalled from long-term storage. For intelligent behaviour to occur, we need to think about, plan, execute and evaluate a specific series of events. We need to store list categories (also called chunks or sequential plans) of specific events in sequence, and then work them into plans that can be carried out later (Grossberg and Pearson, 2008).

This is what working-memory does. It is like a filing clerk in an office, sorting, manipulating and organising items using attention. There is a strong relationship between working-memory and what we call thinking. Prefrontal lobe activity, particularly in the DLPFC in the lateral aspect of the prefrontal cortex, plays a big role. The DLPFC has direct connections to the medial areas associated with emotion and affective behaviour and the VMPFC.

In the chapter on the frontal cortex, we saw how the DLPFC functions near the top of the hierarchy in the mind and plays a large part in working-memory and prolonged and focused attention. These both rely on the ability of the frontal cortex to hold on to and work on information over a period of time.

It takes time to do things. Tasking and goal-related activity requires an ability to plan, to form strategies, to carry them out and then to finish them — activities like science experiments or creating art. It takes time and continuity of thought to experiment and create. This is what working-memory facilitates.

The systems of working-memory monitor what's going on in

our environment. This short-term memory keeps information that is relevant to the situation in mind so that it can be worked on. As the same time as incoming sensory information is being deciphered by other areas of the cortex, there is a relevant depiction of that same information in working-memory, producing something that has meaning for us and is related to our current goals. Because it has meaning and relevance, this analysis, depiction or representation can then be included in real-time into our decision making.

However working-memory is a low capacity memory system, with limited ability to work on and process information and limited storage capacity. It is able to sustain continuous real-time processing depending on the amount of attention available, and seems to be necessary for flexible, abstract and creative thinking and the strategic planning required in carrying out tasks and goals. It also provides access to long-term memory systems and is necessary for the production of consciousness, sentience, perception and our internal narrative.

Working-memory is directly involved with *attention.* The ability to maintain attention is necessary for working-memory to perform effectively, and this seems to be a function of the DLPFC in particular (Dietrich, 2004).

Working-memory is also involved in the conscious assessment and production of our own personal narrative, in rumination and our default mode network. As discussed before, working-memory and attention, along with perception, may be the basis of our internal narrative and perhaps even consciousness itself.

The differences between *working-memory* and *long-term memory* can be shown by comparing what happens when we cook a meal. A lot of the food items we will use have been stored in a pantry ready for use. Like items in long-term memory, these are easily available and ready to be used; they can be stored for a long time, but eventually deteriorate.

Working-memory, on the other hand, is like what happens at the kitchen bench — the powerhouse — where we think, plan and execute: deciding what to take from the pantry, acquiring anything extra, analysing and utilising all the incoming sensory information, such as the temperature of the oven and the freshness of the vegetables, organising and then processing the food items into some sort of edible end-product.

The number of food items on the kitchen bench is much smaller than that available from the pantry or the supermarket. But they can be added to from the pantry at any time, and they are constantly worked on to produce the meal for that evening. After a short period of time, the bench is cleared away ready for the next meal, with little evidence of the previous flurry of activity.

The neural components of working-memory include several subsystems. One processes speech-based verbal information, such as when we rehearse a phone number just given to us. This verbal subsystem has two interactive parts. The first accesses stored verbal knowledge and is associated with activity in the posterior parietal cortex. The second has a rehearsal mechanism that keeps these verbal representations active while we need them and involves Broca's area.

Another subsystem processes visuospatial information, such as the route to the dairy. This subsystem retains mental images of objects and their location in space, and involves the parietal, inferior temporal and occipital cortex.

These two subsystems are co-ordinated by a third subsystem of 'executive control processes', involving the DLPFC and VLPFC, which allocates attentional resources to the other two subsystems, and monitors, manipulates and updates stored representations (Kandel, 2013).

We can see these executive processes happening in real time by using an event-related fMRI (functional MRI). The same 'prefrontal area BA46 of the DLPFC is activated both when subjects select between items on working-memory tasks, and when they freely select between movements on tasks of willed action' (Rowe et al., 2000).

The neural basis of working-memory is relatively simple. It relies on persistent firing of neurons, either by intrinsic mechanisms, such as the opening of calcium channels to maintain persistent firing, or by network connections. The efficiency of working-memory and persistence of activity in prefrontal cortical neurons also depends on the activation of D1 dopamine receptors. Defects of the regulation of working-memory in the frontal cortex by these receptors are thought to contribute to schizophrenia (Kandel, 2013).

Epiphanies have a close relationship to working-memory. When an epiphany happens, such as those of Kary Mullis or Jean Hoerni referred to earlier, information is chunked onto our working-memory bench, cued by current circumstances — such as when we are relaxed with our needs satisfied and 'in the groove' just thinking about things — and restored from available portions of long-term memory. This produces a mishmash of information that finally crystallises in a moment that our emotions can relate to, as Herbert Simon would say, 'satisficing' us. This moment of epiphany will remain clear and accessible for about two hours or so until it is replaced. After that, the train of thought that led to the epiphany is a lot harder to access.

So if a bright idea pops into your head, record it, or make a hard copy as soon as you can. Dictate a memo, write it down or type a note. Many writers have pen and paper beside their beds for those annoying nocturnal epiphanies that are so easily forgotten by morning.

List recall — an example of working-memory and what affects it

Sophisticated models of how the lateral prefrontal cortex works have been proposed by combining information from psychological studies with information from neuroscience.

'How does the brain carry out working-memory storage, categorisation, and voluntary performance of event sequences?' ask Grossberg and Pearson. To answer this question they produced a complex neural model called LIST PARSE — Laminated Integrated Storage of Temporal Patterns for Associative Retrieval, Sequencing and Execution.

The model suggests how 'laminated circuits of lateral prefrontal cortex carry out working-memory storage of event sequences within layers 6 and 4'. These 'event sequences are unitised through learning into list chunks within layer 2/3', and 'these stored sequences can be recalled at variable rates that are under volitional control by the basal ganglia'. The model clarifies why spatial and non-spatial working-memories share the same type of circuit design.

This model is partly based on studies of recall that look at how we retrieve from recent memory the items that have been presented in a list, and what affects that retrieval.

Two tests of recall have been used in many studies:

1. Tests of immediate free recall (IFR), in which lists can be recalled out of sequence
2. Tests of immediate serial recall (ISR), where lists have to be recalled in sequence. These tests can be done to show how different conditions affect both the number of items recalled and how recall is related to their position in the list. For instance, in tests of serial recall, the last items do tend to be recalled last. But, and this may seem counter-intuitive, in tests of free recall, the last items are often not recalled first.

A serial performance curve can be produced if we graph the number of times an item is recalled against their position in the list. These curves show that the first and last items are recalled most, with those in the middle being recalled least. This has led to the terms 'primacy effect' and 'recency effect'. The primacy effect is where the *first* items are remembered more often, and the recency effect is where the *last*, or most recent, items are recalled more often. These effects can be enhanced or diminished depending on a number of factors.

For instance, the last item is remembered more often, showing an increased recency effect, if the subject's attention is diverted *during* the task. But if the subject's attention is distracted *after* the task, the last item is remembered less often, showing a decreased recency effect. The last item is remembered more often if the lists are presented at a faster rate and as sound rather than pictures. The first item on the list is remembered more often, an increased primacy effect, when there is more time between the presentation and the recall of the list.

There are a number of interesting conditions that affect the length, or 'span', of the lists that subjects can recall correctly. Those with more items or those containing words that take longer to say (e.g. words with more syllables) tend to be less commonly recalled than lists with fewer items or shorter words. Recall performance is worse with a list composed of items that are phonologically confusing (e.g. rhyming letters B, D, C and G), than it is with lists of less-confusing content.

The number of items recalled increases when more non-words that sound like words are presented, and is not influenced by subvocal rehearsal. Item familiarity increases the maximum number of items recalled. Items that are less familiar are effectively recalled when they are presented in lists of other less familiar, or weak, items. In contrast, strong items are not recalled as well in pure-strong lists than in mixed lists.

How fast the words on the list are spoken when presented — the articulation rate — affects recall, and the number of words recalled is directly related to the articulation rate. When pauses are inserted between groups of items, primacy and recency gradients within groups are created. Increasing the time before rehearsing the list reduces the number of items recalled, and delays as small as two to three seconds can make remembering the whole list impossible. Surprisingly, memory for some portions of the lists may persist for much longer intervals, sometimes weeks (Grossberg and Pearson, 2008).

This has major implications in how we remember information from lectures or phone calls. If you want to remember something, the most important thing to do is to record it quickly before you forget it because, no matter how good you think you are, you are likely to remember only some of the first and last bits of information. This also has major implications for how we should present information for it to have maximum effect, and it helps to explain cognitive effects such as 'illusions of remembering' and the 'availability heuristic' as described by Tversky and Kahneman in 1974.

When we lecture, we can determine beforehand what we want our students to remember, knowing that on average three items per lecture are remembered. Then we can determine what items we present first, middle and last, using small lists, spacing the familiar items amongst the less familiar, the strong amongst the weak, pausing regularly with distractions and presenting important items before the distractions.

If we are involved in business, it is important to realise that new customers will remember their first and last impressions most. So whatever their first point of contact, make it memorable and enjoyable, and when they leave, let them go away with a positive memory so they will come back.

In medical practice, patients having to endure a horrible waiting room and seeing a grumpy doctor too busy to say goodbye properly may, understandably, feel annoyed, complain and then go somewhere else next time. And if things do go pear-shaped in the middle of a consultation, ending on a happy note may make the patient's memory of the consultation more positive. It is worth remembering that a patient will take away, on average, only three facts from any consultation, unless things are written down.

Long-term memory processes

Long-term memory is such an important part of who we are, what we do and why we do it. This type of memory is important to consciousness and to the development and maintenance of our sense of self and internal narrative. It is used when we recognise an object, when we create, when we imagine and when we plan. Long-term memory acts as an important reference from the past, signposting our future.

For any long-term memory to be formed, information about the event or object needs to be heeded to using attention, acquired, then translated or encoded, and then consolidated or stabilised for long-term storage and ready recall. Most memory forms need attention in order to be *acquired* but may not need attention to be *recalled*.

Two sets of terms have been used to describe various memory processes:

- Those of implicit, non-declarative, automatic or subconscious memory
- Those of explicit, declarative, non-automatic or conscious memory.

In this section the terms *implicit* and *subconscious*, as well as the terms *explicit* and *conscious* are used interchangeably.

- ***Subconscious memory*** systems generally operate automatically, with little use of attention in recall
- ***Conscious memory*** operates under voluntary control with varying amounts of attention needed in recall.

Recall of implicit memory is usually related to the conditions in which it is formed, but recall of explicit memory can be recalled under any conditions.

Memory types can be classified in terms of how quickly they can be recalled. Sometimes we need to rapidly assess a situation and have a range of processes that include memory we can use in different situations. For instance, we can use emotion as discussed previously, or priming, or associative memory. With little time available, it helps if we can recall context-specific memories without using the time-sapping facility of attention. These are the memory systems of implicit or subconscious memory.

And if time permits, we need to have a range of memory processes that enable us to be more circumspect and analytical — where the full range of attentional resources can be used to form a more considered, thoughtful opinion. In the range of memory processes described below, those that can be recalled faster are described first.

Implicit, subconscious, long-term memory processes needing minimal or no attention for recall includes those involved in:

- Habituation and sensitisation (non-associative learning)
- Classical and operant conditioning (associative learning)
- Priming

- Procedural memory, used when we acquire new skills and habits.

Explicit, conscious, long-term memory processes using attention for recall include those involved with:

- Semantic memory of facts, people, places and things
- Episodic memory of events (Kandel, 2013).

Over time, recall of some types of memory can shift from being conscious to subconscious. For instance, when we are learning new skills we need to constantly pay attention and recall is conscious. But with further practice, both learning and recall become subconscious, using procedural memory.

Storage is in different sites for different types of memory. Storage of long-term implicit memories requires reflex pathways, including:

- The spinal cord, for habituation and sensitisation
- The amygdala for learned fear
- The neocortex for priming
- The cerebellum for learned motor skills
- The striatum and the basal ganglia for skills and habits.

Storage of long-term explicit memory begins in the hippocampus and other areas in the medial temporal lobe and is then linked to storage areas in the relevant cortex, such as the visual cortex for the visual component of a memory, and Broca's and Wernicke's areas for language (Kandel, 2013).

Habituation and sensitisation — non-associative learning

If our finger touches a hot stove in our kitchen we quickly lift our hand away then jump back and yelp. This is pure reflex action and is the quickest way we have to act. The initial reaction of pulling our hand away is mediated purely through spinal cord reflexes with no initial higher centre involvement. Pain receptors produce nerve impulses that come into the spinal cord and directly connect with the nerves supplying the local muscles. Lucky for us, these then react quickly. We take our hand away.

The yelp comes immediately after, as the signals produced by the strong stimulus move up the spinal cord to reach the brain stem, thalamus, cerebellum and cerebral cortex, producing more complex behaviours such as screaming or swearing or stamping our feet. There has been no learning that leads us to act this way. We are hardwired to do it. Some would say we do it instinctively. This enables us to respond as quickly as we can to danger. But next time we come near the stove, the memory of what happened along with its negative reinforcement, will be recalled from associative memory and hopefully we will be more cautious.

Thus we quickly find out whether a stimulus is weak or strong, harmless or noxious. Continued exposure to a weak single stimulus will reduce our reflex response. We have learned to ignore it. This is called ***habituation***. But if the stimulus is strong or noxious, repeated exposure may increase our response. We have learned to respond to it. This is called ***sensitisation***.

Habituation and sensitisation are two forms of what is called

non-associative learning: the learning involves single stimuli only, without any association with other stimuli or reward and punishment. Different neural pathways are used, and long-term neuronal changes occur in sensitisation, producing a type of memory that is useful to reduce future exposure. Habituation and sensitisation are automatic subconscious activities that don't have to include systems higher in the hierarchy, such as attention, emotion and perception. These important learning processes are very basic indeed.

Habituation

When we think and decide to act, we use information on which to make a decision. Habituation enables us to become efficient information users, sorting out the relevant from the irrelevant. We are hardwired to notice a sudden change in our environment. Sometimes the absolute value of the stimulus is not as important to us as the rate of change of that value.

If that stimulus is perceived to have no benefit and be harmless and nothing changes in our environment, we start ceasing to react and our attention shifts, saving valuable energy. We have learned not to have to react, like we no longer notice the watch on our wrist after wearing it for a while. We have become habituated. Strangely enough, when we stop wearing the watch, it sometimes feels like it's still there on our wrist.

Habituation can be either short or long term.

Short-term habituation results from a reduction in presynaptic transmission caused by a decrease in the number of vesicles being released by the sensory neuron. The supply has simply run out. This then produces a decrease in activation of the interneurons or motor neurons further along the pathway.

In long-term habituation, some synaptic contacts disappear but can reappear with future learning. Not all synapses are affected by habituation, and even small amounts of training can lead to lasting effects. Again, plasticity is pervasive (Kandel, 2013).

Long-term habituation is allied to our innate curiosity. One reason we constantly search for new experience is that over time, if nothing changes, we become habituated: bored, stilted, lifeless. Our mood changes, our frontal lobes shut down, impairing our attention and concentration, and we become less alert and more vulnerable to danger. Most of us don't like being bored: it makes us feel fed up, like that bored, restless teenager who has no outlet for their curiosity, becoming sad, bad or mad.

New experience or change dishabituates us and reawakens us — as the old saying goes, 'a change is as good as a rest'. Sometimes we have to leave our home for a while so we can appreciate it when we return. And we often fall out of love, when familiarity without attraction breeds contempt. Relationships need to be constantly worked at in order for the feelings we call love to survive.

Habituation is also related to consumerism. The shabby 'old' falls out of favour and is confined to the scrapheap, while the sparkling 'new' is venerated and placed on an emotional pedestal. Unfortunately, long-term happiness has nothing to do with shopping. There are obvious pitfalls in the modern context with resource depletion looming. But this behaviour has been around a while. In his 2003 book *Britain BC — Life in Britain and Ireland Before the Romans,* the archaeologist Francis Pryor, after describing the discarded pieces in a Stone Age midden, commented: 'This throwaway culture has been with us a long time indeed ... ' But we can become dishabituated and see things differently. If we start to pay enough attention to our old stuff, it can become new to us again, or if that fails, we can always give away or sell our old stuff for it to become new to someone else.

We also see examples of habituation in the ratcheting up by media of all types — print, television, film and Internet — of violence and imminent crisis in order to generate fear and capture our attention. The levels of violence and fear now needed in order to get our attention in a crowded media space have almost become devoid of emotion. A lot of media has to some extent become unreal. And it's not only violence. The glossy women's mags are constantly using new techniques to reinvent how women are portrayed.

This well-known quote by Jean-Baptiste Alphonse Karr in 1849 is still relevant: '*Plus ça change, plus c'est la même chose*'. Roughly translated it means: 'The more it changes, the more it's the same thing'. The Victorian press alluded to here was well known for its inflammatory remarks, and this behaviour has persisted. In a piece titled 'The idiot culture' for the *New Republic,* the ever-prescient Carl Bernstein suggested that 'increasingly the America rendered today in the American media is illusionary and delusionary'. It is 'disfigured, unreal ... disconnected from the true context of our lives'.

In this piece, he writes that every hour, every day and every week, the media 'covering actually existing American life' continually 'break new ground in getting it wrong'. This 'covenant is distorted by celebrity and the worship of celebrity ... and by the reduction of news to gossip, which is the lowest form of news'. This covenant is also distorted 'by sensationalism, which is always a turning away from a society's real condition; and by a political and social discourse that we — the press, the media, the politicians, *and* the people — are turning into a sewer'.

That was 1992. The press and other media and many politicians, have now geared up a notch. The West is again in an era of post-truth politics, where experts are despised and the emotions of the gutter frame the irrelevance of a lot of current political discourse. Intelligent debate is bullied away by narcissists who think they know it all but who have persistently shown they know nothing relevant.

Fortunately, we will become habituated to them too, so the best way to cope is to enjoy it for the comedy it is. If only it wasn't about such serious issues. We need to realise that all politicians are only there for a limited time. Times will change. Things will pass. Life will go on, hopefully.

Steven Pinker sees the press through a different lens. He frames the news industry as maximising gain from our natural tendency to feel loss more than gain, to feel the negative more than the positive. In one of a flurry of stories in the *Guardian* on the release of his book *Enlightenment Now: The Case for Reason, Science, Humanism, and Progress* published in 2018, Pinker implies that a sense of gloom and doom in the world is easily inflamed by the news policy that can be loosely described as: 'if it bleeds, it leads'.

The 'availability heuristic' is where we assess the probability of an event occurring by how easily examples of the event can be recalled. It arises because of two basic properties of memory:

- that the last remembered is often the first recalled, as in the examples of IFR and ISR
- that information in memory is stored in categories attached to emotion.

The more emotive the memory is, the more it has salience and the more easily it is recalled. If we actually see a house burning, we recall it more often than if we read about it in the newspaper. Fortunately, events that make the news usually have a low likelihood of happening.

Pinker suggests the press has a preference for covering negative events where bleeding leads, and this provides 'an easy formula for pessimists on the editorial page'. Because of the availability heuristic, these negative portrayals become our go-to when thinking about current events, increasing the sense of doom and gloom that prevails, which in turn has a negative influence on our interpretation of events, and so on and so on.

He also floats the idea, with a degree of sarcasm, that all that has to be done by these gatekeepers who are collectively called 'the press' is to 'make a list of all the worst things that are happening anywhere on the planet that week and you have an impressive-sounding — but ultimately irrational — case that civilisation has never faced greater peril'.

This tension and fear are constantly ramped up again and again because we have been seduced into a continual, heightened need to know. By this clever manipulation, habituation is avoided. In 1777, in *The Sorrows of Young Werther,* Johann Wolfgang von Goethe wrote: 'I discovered again that misunderstandings and inertia cause perhaps more to go wrong in this world than slyness and evil intent. In any case, the latter are rarer'. These are wise words that speak to us from so long ago. Yet which is commonly portrayed in the conspiracy theories of today as the most prevalent? Go figure.

Sensitisation

Fundamentally different to habituation, ***sensitisation*** occurs when we are presented with a harmful, noxious, strong stimulus. We have to respond vigorously to any harmful stimulus, and our response results in heightened 'defensive reflexes for withdrawal and escape'. This is part of the fright-and-flight reflex, and we learn to avoid that stimulus next time. These heightened reflexes also extend to other less-harmful stimuli we may come in contact with around the same time, even if we have become habituated to them (Kandel, 2013).

If we have been exposed to a weak stimulus and learnt to ignore it, we become habituated. But we can be sensitised to that weak stimulus if we suddenly receive a strong one. We then become *dishabituated* or *re-sensitised*. For example, if we are continually stroked lightly, we quickly begin to ignore it and soon don't respond. But if we are then pinched, we jump, and if we are then stroked lightly again, we jump as if we have just been pinched (Kandel, 2013).

Sensitisation is more complex than habituation. It produces an increase in synaptic transmission across sensory neurons as well as a variety of interneurons. This is due to changes in neuronal sensitivity, including long-standing changes in chromatin structure and gene expression that give us a more stable memory of noxious stimuli. This makes it easier to differentiate noxious from harmless stimuli, allowing us to respond appropriately in the future. We need to form a stable, long-term memory for things that may do us harm, and we can afford to have a limited memory for stimuli that are basically irrelevant to us (Kandel, 2013).

Classical and operant conditioning — associative learning

Learning refers to a change in behaviour that is a result of 'acquiring knowledge about the world' (Kandel, 2013).

We have seen in the Introduction how complex think real-time thinking — and therefore learning — is. From memory, our habits and beliefs and attitudes about how we should act in different contexts crowd in upon us all the time. Our personality sets the tone, but hunger, pain and emotion, background mood, drugs and sleep, amongst other things, can all affect the ways we think. We are very goal oriented, and these can also be divided into hierarchies — goals and sub-goals, and so on. A goal or sub-goal can be many things and determines how we think.

If our goal is to reach a destination, we problem-solve: we plan how to achieve it, move towards it and constantly assess our progress. Our thinking changes if our goal is to complete a simple task and changes again if we are just free thinking. As well as providing a destination, a goal or sub-goal forms a framework for deciding the relevance of the information we come across. Our conscious state includes our sense of self and a narrative about what the moment we are in actually means — '*Why am I here?*' and '*What am I doing here?*' — and helps to determine how we act.

Two simple models of learning gained traction in the first half of the twentieth century: *classical conditioning* and *operant conditioning*. These are both called associative learning paradigms, because learning results from an association between two things — either two stimuli, or a stimulus and a reward. In these paradigms, it is the change in behaviour that is studied and the brain is the black box in between the presentation of the stimulus and the observed change in behaviour.

Classical conditioning is where an animal learns to change their response to a stimulus, because that stimulus has now been paired or associated with another stimulus. The perception of the new stimulus has been altered by learning about this new association.

Operant conditioning, or reward-based learning, is where a change in behaviour is associated with the presentation of a stimulus that could be either a reward or a punishment. The perception of what the stimulus is hasn't changed — it is still a reward or punishment — but the timing of its presentation induces a change in behaviour that can then be observed.

These types of learning produce implicit memories that can be recalled fast, helping us to be able to interpret and act quickly when we come into contact with new information. This learning takes place consciously, requiring attention for memory to be acquired. Recall does not require attention, and the recalled memory may not enter our consciousness, but it can only be recalled in context. When the light turns green, we go without having to think about it. This is just like when we learn to do something using procedural memory, as we shall see later.

Classical conditioning — Pavlov and his dogs

Classical conditioning is where we have learned an association between two stimuli that enables us to predict future events. In the early twentieth century, the Russian physiologist Ivan Pavlov saw that we often *learn* to respond to a stimulus in a way we wouldn't usually respond. He designed experiments on animals that investigated the learned changes in innate reflex behaviour that resulted from changing relationships between stimuli.

He became interested in this because one day he noticed that as soon as he or his assistant walked into the laboratory, the dogs they were studying began to salivate, something they had never done before. Something had changed, something had been learned. How had this happened? Were the dogs associating his presence with something else?

His classical experiments paired the presentation of a light with the presentation of meat to the dogs. At the start of the experiment, when the dog saw the meat it naturally salivated, but when it saw the light, it wouldn't normally react. In this paradigm, the meat was called the unconditioned stimulus and salivation the unconditioned response.

But after light was paired with the presentation of the meat, the dog's response to it would change, and eventually the light alone would make the animal salivate. The animal had now been conditioned to respond to the light by salivating. The light had become the conditioned stimulus. In this situation, salivation had changed from being an unconditioned response, occurring naturally in response to seeing food, to a conditioned response that had been learned and conditioned to occur when the light was presented. If the light was not presented, salivation would not occur.

Pavlov also studied conditioned fear in dogs. In these studies, an innocuous stimulus such as a buzzer was paired with an aversive stimulus, such as an electric shock that produced a fear-like response in the dog. The buzzer became the conditioned stimulus, so when it was presented again it evoked fear-like behaviours, now called conditioned behaviours, because of its association with an electric shock.

After conditioning, something new had been learned. In the first experiments, presentation of both light and food would make the animal salivate, and the same thing would happen in fear conditioning after presentation of the electric shock and the buzzer. The dogs had learned to respond to a new stimulus in a way they hadn't before. They had become conditioned.

Conditioning was found to be greater when the stimuli were paired close to one another or were contingent upon each other. On the other hand, extinction of the conditioned response could occur if the pairings no longer occurred close together, or were no longer contiguous.

Extinction could also occur if the conditioned stimulus, such as the buzzer, was repeatedly presented without the aversive stimulus. This method is used in cognitive behavioural therapy and exposure therapy. Continued exposure of the patient to a situation or an object that causes anxiety, within the controlled confines of a therapist's office, can reduce the anxiety around that object or situation. This is often called 'facing your fear' (Frankland and Josselyn, 2018).

In our everyday lives we have been so conditioned to respond to stimuli we wouldn't normally respond to. To use a trite example, take the evening news and weather bulletins. By turning on the TV at six o'clock every night to watch the news and weather we get an automatic, unconditioned response. We feel connected. We can discuss what we've seen with other people, enhancing our social interactions. We have satisfied our curiosity for what is happening out there and how it may affect us and we can make plans for tomorrow. For better or for worse, this is our reward.

Now if we set ourselves to regularly turn on the news at 6 pm, after a few days we would notice that just looking at our watch and seeing it is 6 pm would make us feel connected and feel better. The time of 6 pm has become a conditioned stimulus, and the feeling of being connected and aware has become the conditioned response.

Operant conditioning — Skinner and his pigeons

This paradigm of learning, also called instrumental learning or trial-and-error learning was invented by Edward L Thorndike, who observed the behaviour of cats trying to escape from homemade puzzle boxes. The paradigm was expanded by B F Skinner in the mid-twentieth century. *Operant conditioning* involves studying the relationship between the behaviour and its consequences. When a behaviour consistently results in a *positive* reinforcement such as food, it tends to be repeated. When a behaviour consistently results in a *negative* reinforcement or punishment, it tends to be extinguished. Again, timing is important. If the reinforcement does not follow the behaviour quickly, then the conditioning is weak. This is useful — why respond to stimuli that are now associated with no reward or punishment?

We are all under the influence of reinforcement in some way, be it positive or negative. When sitting at the traffic lights we wait expectantly for the lights to turn green. Watching, and waiting. At the green light, a sudden surge of energy rushes through us and off we go. This is our reward for waiting, our positive reinforcement, and we have avoided a negative reinforcement by waiting. Just like pigeons pecking at a green disc to get a reward. And if we do go through a red light, the negative reinforcement, or punishment, can be severe.

Once we have learned these associations, they can be used to interpret current stimuli and help us decide what to do. Most of us do stop at traffic lights when they turn red. Most of us have learned to dress appropriately in certain situations. Failure to do so would lead to negative consequences, such as a traffic fine or accident, or criticism from the people around us.

There can be other effects. After we have received a reward associated with a particular behaviour, it is easy to form a superstition that the reward will always follow this behaviour. Later, we may then repeat the same behaviour hoping for the same reward. Unfortunately, most of us don't pay attention to a concept called 'regression to the mean'. Forming beliefs and superstitions based on one event may not be very useful.

Values describing any one event should not be interpreted in isolation. 'Regression to the mean' is a statistical term that suggests that all values describing an event will trend towards the mean value for that variable when it is measured again. So the initial information we have about an event, such as a reward following a particular behaviour, may be so far off the mark that we need subsequent information to decide whether this information is relevant. We need to determine where does the mean for this event occur?

Not understanding this concept of 'regression to the mean' can lead us to overestimate the effectiveness of punishment, and to underestimate the effectiveness of reward. Consider an event that produces results that can lead to punishment or reward, such as behaviour in a school classroom. If behaviour is 'bad', it leads to punishment. Then if the behaviour is better next time, we think the punishment has been effective.

But by natural chance, the next result can trend more towards the mean. That is, the behaviour will get better anyway. We have wrongly attributed the improvement in behaviour to the punishment. In other words, we have overestimated the effectiveness of the punishment. Also, when behaviour is 'good' and a reward is given, the next result can trend towards the mean and be worse. We will then say the reward is unlikely to improve results, and we will have underestimated the effectiveness of the reward (Tversky and Kahneman, 1974).

Culture is part of context and plays a large part in reward. Culture conditions us by continuously reinforcing behaviour according to the beliefs of that culture. It is one of the ways culture constantly influences how we think and what we decide.

One of the simplest ways to remember the differences between classical and operant conditioning is to focus on whether the behaviour is involuntary or voluntary.

- Classical conditioning is passive and entails making an association between an *involuntary* response and a stimulus.
- Operant conditioning is active and is about making an association between a *voluntary* behaviour and a consequence.

In operant conditioning, the learner is also rewarded with incentives, while classical conditioning involves no such enticements.

Both classical and operant conditioning can be used in a variety of situations by many people, such as teachers, parents, psychologists and animal trainers. An animal trainer may use classical conditioning by repeatedly pairing the sound of a clicker with the taste of food. Eventually, the sound of the clicker alone will begin to produce the same response the taste of food would. In a classroom, a teacher might use operant conditioning by offering tokens as rewards for good behaviour. Students can turn in these tokens to receive some type of reward, such as a treat or extra play time.

Why do we quickly spit out food that has made us sick in the past, so-called 'taste aversion'? Taste aversion in humans doesn't develop if the side effect of the food is pain not nausea, and it develops only with some foods. And animals don't develop aversion to auditory or visual stimuli that are paired with nausea (Kandel, 2013). Conditioning can also help explain some other behaviours: Why do we get aroused when we smell our partner? Where does the power of prayer come from? Why do babies smile when we make those silly cooing noises?

In research, these paradigms of learning can also be used to show that bees really can learn (Alem et al., 2016).

The systems involved in reward

Different neural systems generally use only one type of neurotransmitter. Neurons using dopamine as their transmitter are involved in both anticipation and recognition of reward and in avoiding adverse events. This neural system, often called the 'reward circuit', includes the ventral tegmental area in the midbrain and its projections onto the nucleus accumbens, the amygdala and the medial prefrontal cortex. This circuit is also known as the mesolimbic pathway. Its role in reward was discovered when it was shown that rodents would actively seek electrical stimulation in these brain regions.

These regions were also found to overlap with the distribution of dopaminergic neurons and their projection onto the prefrontal cortex and nucleus accumbens. Studies where opiates or nicotine were injected into these pathways leading to positive reinforcement, confirmed they were involved in pleasure. These reward centres also include parallel opposing circuits that can produce either reward or punishment, where some dopaminergic neurons respond to noxious stimuli (Fields, 2014).

Dopaminergic systems produce complex effects. They have a role as a feedback signal for predicting rewards. A surge of dopamine signals is produced when we are successful in obtaining a reward, and also when we have an uncomfortable near miss. The dopaminergic system is signalling how close we got to a reward and encourages us to do it again. This is useful if success relies on skill but is unhelpful when it depends on chance.

These systems also help to support our motivation to avoid unpleasant experiences. If traumatised war veterans are reminded of the sounds of battle, which naturally they find abhorrent, they produce surges of dopamine in the nucleus accumbens. Dopaminergic neurons are also included in pathways that regulate movement in the substantia nigra and attention in the frontal cortex (Bell, 2013).

Other neural systems using serotonin are concerned with behaviour associated with reward. Serotonin is produced by several groups of neurons in the brain stem such as the locus coeruleus and the raphe nucleus which have many connections to the higher centres, mainly in the cerebral cortex, in a similar way to the ventral tegmental area. A more detailed description is in the Definitions section in Part Two.

Serotonergic systems have been implicated in the regulation of mood states, including depression, anxiety, food intake and aggressive behaviour. Reduced serotonergic activity lowers our threshold for violence, increases our appetite, lowers our mood and increases our anxiety. So, systems using serotonin can influence behaviours that lead to reward or punishment (Kandel, 2013).

Priming

Priming is an interesting psychological concept that affects the many processes involved in our perception of self and the world around us. It subconsciously uses episodic and semantic memory, and occurs when exposure to a cue influences a response to a later cue. It can occur following either a perceptual, semantic or conceptual cue. It is another reason why many commentators have suggested there is no such thing as free will.

Whether we have free will or freedom of choice is a complex question that has been debated for a long time in philosophy. On the surface, some of the neuroscience suggests that sometimes we may not. Free will and freedom of choice imply a conscious effort is needed when we make a choice of 'this' or 'that'. In priming, subconscious access to memory can definitely influence the decisions we make.

Say we have two groups of people — those who have read a list of words including the word 'table', and those who haven't. They are all later asked to complete a word starting with 'tab'. The people who have read the list will answer 'table' more often than the people who have not read the list and have not been 'primed'.

The effects of priming can be strong and long-lasting, even more so than simple recognition memory. Subconscious priming effects can affect word choice in word-stem completion tests long after the words have been consciously forgotten. A quick glance at a billboard advertising can prime us to buy something months later. In the 1962 film *The Manchurian Candidate,* the character Sergeant Raymond Shaw has been brainwashed in captivity and primed to kill if he receives a particular message.

Priming works best when the two cues are in the same modality. For example, visual priming works best with visual cues; verbal priming works best with verbal cues. But priming also occurs between modalities or between semantically related words, such as 'doctor' and 'nurse' (Wikipedia, accessed December 2017).

Priming is not restricted to concepts or words and can occur within many domains of life. Our actions can be primed by events we are not even aware of. We have seen the study by Zhu in 2015, in the previous section on emotion. Here participants were primed to think of emotional concepts after being exposed to emotional stimuli.

In 2011, Kahneman referred to priming in one of his many studies as the 'ideomotor effect'. Students aged 18 to 22 were asked to form four-word sentences from a set of five words. When that was completed, the students were asked to walk down a corridor to another experiment, and the time it took them to do that was secretly measured. Some students were given groups of words to look at that contained a theme relating to older people, and they took longer to walk down than students who had not been exposed to those words. Using words relating to an older age group produced behaviours that mimicked this group.

This has relevance for 'senior citizens' in our large gated communities, living in 'homes for the aged'. Constant exposure to aged behaviour *produces* aged behaviour, as we mimic the behaviour of those around us. But aged behaviour relates more to attitude than to birth date. Baring disability, if you think you are old and live amongst older people, you will be primed to behave as if you are old. It's a good reason for maintaining an extended family. Being involved with younger people — children, grandchildren, students and friends — keeps older people looking and acting younger. And it's important for the younger. It gives them perspective and teaches them respect and caring.

Procedural memory

Procedural memory is what we use when we do things we have done before. In situations of routine tasking, we use procedural memory which is largely implicit (subconscious, non-declarative and automatic). Procedural memory can be acquired *subconsciously* for simple tasks demanding minimal attention, and *consciously* for more complex tasks that demand more attention. Using procedural memory without needing conscious effort saves us time and energy in routine tasks, such as cooking and cleaning, mowing lawns, training for a sport. Or other routine tasks, such as driving on an empty road that we know well, in good conditions with a silent passenger, or shutting the front door in a rush to get to work.

Procedural memory allows us to do more than one thing at once, but multitasking can only work when the tasks performed need low levels of attention, use different bits of the nervous system or are able to be performed over different time periods. We can check our emails while texting and talking hands-free on the phone. But it is difficult to quickly write an email and text at the same time. As soon as we need to be attentive to a particular task, we stop doing everything else. Loss of procedural memory is suspected when people lose old skills or are unable to learn new ones.

Procedural memory uses the memory of the cerebellum and

its cortex, the hippocampus and the information-processing of the basal ganglia and supplementary motor cortex and their connections to motor neurons, to produce the subconscious actions. There may be little connection to the conscious, to the frontal cortex. When using procedural memory, we may act but not remember.

When thinking about the last part of a journey in the car or after leaving the house in a hurry, we often can't remember doing what we've obviously just done. That's good use of procedural memory. Older people often think this is because they are 'getting old' or developing Alzheimer's, but it isn't. It is a normal use of procedural memory. No attention was needed, saving energy, and the events were not transferred to conscious memory.

But if that person in the passenger seat suddenly starts talking when we are driving down that empty road, then we pay more attention. Our brain becomes more active, we slow down, frown, our pupils dilate, and we will ultimately remember what we have just done. We are still using our procedural memory to drive the car but with increased attention produced by the conversation. This increased attention will result in a memory being acquired for what we have just done. We will then be able to remember the parts of the journey we were paying attention to.

Conscious long-term memory processes

Conscious or explicit or declarative memories are those recalled consciously using attention, so the memory becomes part of the conscious state when it's remembered. Most of us, when asked what memory is, would think of conscious memory.

What are memories made of and where do they exist?

Plato suggested they are like impressions formed by our thoughts and perceptions on a block of wax within our soul, and that we can remember these thoughts and perceptions as long as the impressions they form have not been erased. This analogy shows some of the properties of long-term memory — some are transient and soon forgotten, and some are stable and long-lasting and easily recalled. But all are plastic and malleable (Draghun, 2018).

For a conscious long-term memory to be formed, information has to first be acquired, then encoded and consolidated for long-term storage. It can be recalled at any time and any stage. But long-term, consciously recalled memories are not like never-changing videos that we can replay over and over again.

A recalled memory rarely brings back the total experience of the time. Koestler described them as 'skeletonised visual generalisations'. Conscious memories constantly change, gnawed at by time like a moth-eaten blanket. When retrieved, they are reconstructed in context but then the details, 'even shadows ... and all but the crudest forms of colour ... are usually absent from visual memories' (Koestler, 1967).

And *memory and emotion* interact. Usually a past event associated with a strong emotion, such as anger, fear, love or hate, will be remembered more easily than an event associated with little emotion, that has little emotional valence.

And *memory and time* interact. It can take months for memories to be consolidated into long-term memory and only milliseconds for them to be recalled. And they change. Like everywhere in the brain, plasticity is pervasive. Revisiting the places we have experienced before then modifies the old memories of those places into something new. Childhood memories are often changed if we return to the places where we grew up.

Long-term memories which are recalled consciously are intertwined series of portions of events we have experienced, often encoded over many different brain regions in distributed networks, called engrams. The term engram was first used in the early twentieth century by a German zoologist, Richard Semon, to describe the physical nature of a memory in the brain.

In 1949, the Canadian physiologist Donald Hebb proposed that during learning, repeated stimulation strengthens the synaptic connections between neurons. 'Neurons that fire together, wire together' is his famous phrase. It is thought that these stimulated neurons then become coactive, forming scattered populations of distinct groups of neurons that undergo changes in the structure and function of their connections. These groups of neuronal assemblies have been called engrams, ensembles or memory traces.

To produce these engrams, experience as information is translated and *acquired, encoded* and then *consolidated* for *storage*.

Where do these engrams exist? The number of sites where storage occurs depends on the type of memory but is potentially infinite. Most of the information is stored in long-term association-areas in the cortex that maintain links or traces with the prefrontal cortex and hippocampus, where the engram is probably first formulated.

Acquisition and encoding

For information to be laid down in memory, we first have to acquire it. For *acquisition* to occur, we need to pay attention to and then interpret this information using perception. The processes around 'acquiring' producing an interpretation of information — called a percept — will be discussed in the next chapter. It seems logical that a percept is essentially an initial engram.

How we perceive depends partly upon our mood, the time available and our social context. The emotional value or valence of what's being memorised also influences how well that memory is laid down at the time, and how well it can be recalled later. Those long, moist kisses at golden sunsets with our first love are easily remembered because of the intense emotions involved. Memories of unrequited love and the associated sense of something lost can also produce strong feelings, again because of the emotion involved.

And repetition enhances acquisition. The more often something is repeated, the more likely we are to remember it. This is valuable in the propaganda of election campaigns where simple messages repeated often help candidates to win. And how often do we see candidates who don't stay on message lose?

Within the brain, acquisition of a memory starts with the hippocampus. Other central structures associated with acquisition and encoding that facilitate long-term memory storage are the entorhinal cortex, the dentate region and other areas of the medial temporal lobe such as the subiculum. A detailed description of the hippocampus and surrounding areas is in the Glossary in Part Two.

Patients with various brain lesions have also given insights into the structures involved in memory processes. Like Phineas Gage with his injury to the frontal cortex, Henry Molaison was one of the first patients who provided insights into the role of the hippocampus in memory. He was known only as HM until his passing in December 2008 at the age of 82. When he was seven years old, he had a bicycle accident that resulted in intractable temporal lobe epilepsy. His seizures meant that he could not work or lead a normal life. So at 27, he had surgery to remove the anterior two thirds of his hippocampus and nearby regions in the medial temporal lobes, including the parahippocampus, the entorhinal cortex and the amygdala on both sides.

The surgery helped his epilepsy, but he developed 'a devastating memory deficit'. He still had normal working-memory for up to a few minutes, as his DLPFC was not affected, a good recall for events that had occurred before the operation, a good vocabulary and an unchanged IQ. But he could not transfer new information from short-term working-memory into long-term memory, particularly if distracted. 'He was unable to retain for lengthy periods information about people, places or objects that he had just encountered'. He was repeatedly unable to recognise the psychologist Brenda Milner when they continued to meet, even though she had seen him every month for some time (Kandel, 2013).

Once information is acquired, it is then encoded over many different brain regions to produce an engram, a single record of a particular experience. Little is known about how encoding happens, but it is spread over wide areas of association cortex.

Consolidation and storage

Consolidation is where new memories that are still quite labile are stabilised (Ramirez, 2018; Frankland and Josselyn, 2018).

The hippocampus is central to most long-term memory processes like the hub on a wheel, but it cannot contain the enormous amount of information our memories hold. Its role is similar to some of the functions of the central processing unit in a computer. It receives, processes and then sends information to and from storage sites. Its purpose appears to be to assemble information after it has been acquired and code it into an early, distinct engram. This engram is further consolidated for long-term storage in a network of neocortical sites.

Long-term links between the cortical storage sites and the hippocampus are formed and sporadically activated, strengthening long-term storage and easy recall. The hippocampus may be involved in recalling these stored memories in a coherent fashion, acting as a link between the searching prefrontal cortex on the one hand, and the cortical storage sites on the other. It behaves a bit like the librarian you asked to find a book you want, or when you click on the links on a web page. But Henry Molaison has shown us that some long-term memories can be recalled without hippocampal activation. It may be that recall of memories from long ago may be more dependent on the frontal cortex than the hippocampus.

Once these relevant representations have been transferred to a widespread neocortical network and a stable, long-term representation of the engram is formed, the hippocampus is cleared of all but a trace, a link back. This enables more memories to be formed. Sleep may play a large role in this resetting of the hippocampus to make it ready for the production of new memories when we awake in the morning (Draguhn, 2018).

Newly formed memory in neocortical regions is plastic but becomes more stable over time. The time it takes to stabilise into a storable long-term version is currently unknown, but it appears to be less than three hours. A study of visual perception learning (VPL) using real-time magnetic resonance spectroscopy has shown that the plastic stage of memory consolidation correlates well with the release of the excitatory neurotransmitter glutamine and that this release declines over time. Release of the inhibitory neurotransmitter γ-aminobutyric acid (GABA) is associated with a decrease in plasticity and an increase in stability (Ji et al., 2018).

This study also compared the time for reconsolidation after recall of a previous memory and found it to be the same as consolidation of new memory. This shows that after old memories are recalled, there is a period of time when they become labile again, just as they were when they were first formed. This means they can then be changed before being reconsolidated. This is why our childhood memories are changed when we revisit places where we grew up. We recall those old memories then add new details before they are reconsolidated. When we recall them again later on, they have been changed to include the new information.

After this initial instability during consolidation, long-term engram stability can be produced by a variety of mechanisms. Working-memory is thought to depend on persistent neural firing, whereas initial long-term explicit memory storage after consolidation is related to the strength of the synaptic connections, or long-term potentiation (LTP).

The storage of explicit memory involves different forms of LTP in the hippocampus, with an early and a late phase, and can be associative or non-associative, depending on the pathways activated. For instance, LTP in one of the input pathways, the Schaffer collateral pathway, is associative. It can only occur in association with stimulation of the postsynaptic membrane at the same time. This is a possible mechanism for producing memory in classical conditioning. LTP in another pathway, the mossy fibre pathway, is non-associative. Early LTP lasts up to three hours and depends on strong, presynaptic neuronal firing with no change in gene transcription (Kandel, 2013).

But long-term memory would be impossible if it depended on continual neuronal firing. A later stage of long-memory consolidation depends on long-term depression (LTD) of synaptic transmission. The early stage of LTP is induced with a burst of high-frequency stimulation, but LTD is induced by long periods of low-frequency stimulation that may periodically refresh the links that form the memory (Kandel, 2013).

Donald Hebb also suggested there may be other ways of storing long-term consolidated memories. As well as the well-known 'neurons that fire together, stay together', he thought that some 'growth processes or metabolic change' happens when an axon of cell A repeatedly excites cell B 'so that A's efficiency as one of the cells firing B is increased'.

To store consolidated memories, there must be some long-term changes in cell function. Normal cellular processes in the neuron are heavily dependent on proteins, which include the release of neurotransmitters and maintenance and activation of the postsynaptic receptors. There are also various signalling cascades within the cell that can affect gene transcription and protein synthesis. Since the 1960s, the processes around gene transcription and protein synthesis have been thought to be behind the molecular changes in cell function that produce a lasting memory trace.

Within the neuron, the long strands of base pairs that make up DNA lie in the nucleus of the cell body, but the DNA needs to be compacted upon itself to be able to fit within the confines of the nucleus. To do this, the 164 base pair units of DNA strands are coiled around an eight-sided histone protein to form a nucleosome. These nucleosomes then bind together with another histone to form a chromatin complex. This chromatin complex containing the DNA is called the epigenome. It can exist in two forms — an open form where the DNA is accessible, and a closed restrictive form.

The DNA within the nucleus provides the template for the production of proteins within the cell by a process called transcription. The proteins that are made usually last for only a few hours, but the DNA must be accessible for transcription to occur.

Epigenetic changes, such as DNA methylation and histone modification, can shift the chromatin complex from closed to open states, allowing transcription to take place and new proteins to be made. DNA methylation can be a stable and self-perpetuating mechanism for sustaining epigenetic changes that are heritable over generations of the cell. It is likely to be one factor involved in the long-term changes in protein production that enable stable memory formation (Kandel, 2013).

We know there are changes to gene expression in consolidation of memory, but how these changes promote memory consolidation is currently unknown. There is a suggestion that changes in neurotransmitter production and release, and the formation and modification of receptors is involved. This could also support the consolidation of long-term memory and reconsolidation after recall (Zovkic, 2013).

Thus the magic that is DNA is involved in long-term memory processes in the neuron at a fundamental level. It stores both long-standing evolutionary changes and the more recent changes related to our own experiences.

Studies of particular types of memory have also given insights into memory processes around consolidation and storage. One type of memory that has been well studied in hippocampal networks in rats is that of spatial memory.

In 1971, it was discovered that the rat hippocampus contains a 'cognitive map' of its spatial environment. There are special neurons, called place cells, in the CA3 and CA1 regions of the hippocampus that become activated when the animal is in a certain spot of its environment, called the cell's place field. Then, when the animal moves to a different environment, other neurons are activated and these form new place fields that can be stable up to months. Recording the electrical activity in a number of place fields can then predict where the animal is in its environment, hence the term 'cognitive map' (Kandel, 2013).

While exploring an environment, place cells are activated in sequence, and their coupling is strengthened. These coactive couplings then form neuronal ensembles like engrams, and more of these couplings are formed with further experience. Recordings of electrical activity show the local membrane-potential oscillations that represent the initial engrams of this spatial experience (Draghun, 2018).

The long-term stability of a neuron's place field also depends on attention. When a mouse walks through a space it is not paying attention to, the place fields form but are unstable after around three to six hours. If a mouse is foraging for food and paying attention to where it is, the place fields that are formed can be stable for days (Kandel, 2013).

Stabilisation of these sequences of place cell activity happens during periods of immobility or deep sleep. This is also known as slow-wave sleep, or non-REM (rapid eye movement) sleep. In 2018, Norimoto showed two properties of slow-wave sleep in mice: 1) that hippocampal networks produce spontaneous SWR activity, and 2) that the synaptic coupling strength between some hippocampal neurons declines.

In deep slow-wave sleep, the spatial sequences formed during the day are replayed in the same order in the hippocampus. But a much faster pattern of network oscillations, called hippocampal sharp-wave ripples (SWRs), are seen when this is happening. These are different to the initial local membrane-potential oscillations seen during acquisition. Some excitatory synapses are weakened in the hippocampus during this SWR activity.

These hippocampal SWRs happen at the same time as similar activity in prefrontal and parietal association-cortex, suggesting co-ordinated activity during consolidation in widespread interconnected cortical networks. In turn, hippocampal SWRs are themselves influenced by ongoing cortical oscillations (Khodagholy, 2017).

During deep sleep, the coupling activity of place cells in the hippocampus representing old, well-known environments declines, whereas recently formed couplings remain active. This separates the newly formed engrams from older engrams and may help to maintain plasticity in the network during future experiences. The underlying cellular and molecular mechanisms are typical for an activity-dependent synaptic plasticity (Norimoto, 2018; Draghun, 2018).

Retrieval

Storage and retrieval of explicit memory also relies on the ability to distinguish between two sets of similar information, such as images or episodes or spatial configurations. This is called pattern separation. It is useful when we need to determine if the differences between these two sets of information are important.

On recall, partial sets of information, or cues, can be used to retrieve memory. These cues can trigger the filling in of an incomplete memory by a process called pattern completion. Here the retrieval process doesn't have to wait until all information has been analysed. It makes a best guess that attempts to fit what we perceive with what we know, to quickly form an interpretation. It is also useful if there is only a partial set of cues with which to recall. In medicine, this happens all the time, where partial sets of information are used to make a guess about a patient's condition (Kandel, 2013).

Retrieval for recall is a constructive process similar to perception, which is partly dependent on working-memory and can be distorted according to time, emotion and context. We use a variety of cognitive strategies during retrieval that include:

'comparison, inference, shrewd guessing and supposition'. This generates 'a memory that not only seems coherent to us but is also consistent with other memories and with our "memory of the memory"' (Kandel, 2013).

Imperfections of memory from studies of 'forgetting and distortion' have been called the 'seven sins of memory'. These are: 'transience, absent-mindedness, blocking, misattribution, suggestibility, bias and persistence'. At present, little is known about many of the processes that cause these observed errors (Schacter, 2001).

Absent-mindedness and blocking are referred to as problems of **omission**, when stored memory is temporarily inaccessible.

Absent-mindedness, such as forgetting where we recently placed an object, or forgetting to pick up something on the way home from work, is produced by a lack of attention that is needed to form the initial engram during encoding. This may be normal though, if we have forgotten where we placed an object because we were using procedural memory.

Blocking is where there is a temporary lack of access to stored information, where it is 'on the tip of the tongue' but unable to be accessed fully. Functional MRI studies in people who have entered this 'on-the-tip-of-the-tongue' state have shown intense activity in the anterior cingulate cortex (ACC) and right DLPFC'. These are areas that we have seen are concerned with decision-making and working-memory (Maril et al., 2001).

Errors of memory can also be characterised as problems of **commission**, where some form of memory is present but it is wrong.

Misattribution is when a memory is falsely associated with the wrong time, place or person. Studies using fMRI and PET have shown similar levels of activity in the hippocampus during 'true and false recognition, which may be one reason why false memories sometimes feel like real ones'.

Suggestibility is where external information is incorporated into existing memory, 'usually as a result of leading questions or suggestions'. Studies with young adults have shown that 'repeated suggestions to imagine a childhood experience can produce memories of experiences that never occurred'. Hypnotic suggestion in susceptible people can also produce false memories.

Bias refers to 'distortions and unconscious influences on memory that reflect one's general knowledge and beliefs'. This is when people often misremember to 'make it consistent with what they presently believe, know or feel'.

Persistence 'refers to obsessive memory, constant remembering of information or events that we might want to forget', such as occurs in people with post-traumatic stress disorder. As we have seen, encoding and retrieval of persistent emotional memories involve both the amygdala and the hippocampal formation (Kandel, 2013).

Episodic memory

How do we instantly recognise an angry face or a happy face? How do we recognise a threatening person when we are out walking the streets? Here we are using 'episodic memory'. Episodic memory is an explicit (and conscious, declarative and non-automatic) memory system of personal experiences — the who, why, what and where of one's life.

These are the memories of faces, of what was bought at the supermarket yesterday, or the joke Grandpa told at the dinner table. 'Flash-bulb memory' is a special part of episodic memory that stores emotional events linked to where we were at the time these events happened. Where were we when 9/11 occurred, or when Princess Diana died, or when JFK was shot? We may not remember day-to-day details of our past, but what we do remember is often linked to the strong emotions felt at the time.

We have a large database of faces in our memory. Faces are among the first groups of stimuli, or cues, we come in contact with. Some would say we are hardwired to remember them, but we are using episodic memory gained from experience and often associated with reward. The look on our father's face when he made cooing noises to extract a smile. And then our smile is rewarded with a barrage of hugs, making us do it again. The hugs reinforce the smile. Reward has changed our behaviour, and we have stored this in our episodic memory.

We soon get to know that faces convey lots of information, some of it very useful. We want to know if Dad is angry in order to run away and hide, and escape the inevitable punishment. We want to know whether the stranger in the train late at night is friendly or threatening. We want to know what the driver in that car is going to do next. Alex Todorov at Princeton University has shown that, in a single glance at a human face, we can determine whether the face is hostile or threatening, how dominant it is and whether it can be trusted or not. The fusiform gyrus in the inferior temporal lobe is heavily involved in facial recognition (Kahneman, 2011; Todorov, 2009).

Semantic memory

If we are asked to fill in the next numbers in a sequence of say, 2, 4, 6 ... we are using semantic memory. Semantic memory is a general store of conceptual and factual knowledge unrelated to personal memory. Its use is explicit (and conscious, declarative and non-automatic) and involves the association areas of the medial and lateral temporal cortex, the prefrontal cortex, the hippocampus and the thalamus.

These memories include knowledge of words and numbers, or the colour of fog on a misty morning, or the name of a Greek philosopher. They are context-free facts that can be verbalised. Semantic memory is enhanced by repetition, such as when learning names, and can be quickly recalled in response to the appropriate cue. When we recognise someone in the street we often don't have to think about what their name is — it just comes to us.

Truisms such as the phrase: 'when you hear hoof beats think horses not zebras' (unless of course you're on the African savannah), relate to semantic memory. We also use semantic memory for sequences of numbers, using our frontal lobes a bit more, often very briefly. This time we have to concentrate on the question, figure out what it means and rapidly search our memory to come up with an answer. Semantic memory is stored differently to episodic memory. We can have a severe loss of episodic memory while our semantic memory remains intact.

Summary — a theory of long-term memory

It has become possible to think of explicit long-term memory as being a result of several stages of neural activity. A simplified basic scheme could work something like this:

Information from our senses is initially processed at receptor level in the periphery. It then passes into the dorsal horn of the spinal cord for further modification. This modified information is projected up the spinal cord into structures like the thalamus where it is further modified. Next, the resulting highly modified information is projected onto the primary and association areas of the cortex and the DLPFC, where a working representation is formed. This is finally projected onto the entorhinal cortex.

As we shall see in the next chapter, this is also the process of perception, where incoming sensation is modified and formed into a percept. This percept is an interpretation or working representation of what the sensory information actually means.

The entorhinal cortex is a link between the hippocampus and the rest of the brain. It receives the highly processed inputs of every sensory modality from areas of association cortex as well as inputs related to ongoing cognitive processes via the prefrontal cortex. It possibly receives the percept at the time it is formed.

As well as highly processed information, it also receives inputs from brain stem nuclei, such as the locus coeruleus and raphe nuclei that affect arousal and mood, and nuclei within the thalamus and hypothalamus that produce our feelings. The output to the hippocampus is via the perforant pathway.

Other inputs to the hippocampus come from the dopamine, serotonin and noradrenalin systems directly, as well as from the medial septal nucleus. These inputs modulate the activity of the hippocampus and determine what is remembered.

These inputs could also be attached to the modified sensory information of the percept to produce a network of tagged neurons linked to the hippocampus. This tagged network would include the modified sensory information of the percept along with the associated feelings at the time. It could form the initial engram or memory trace. So it could be that an engram is basically a modified percept.

Outputs from the hippocampus go largely to the entorhinal cortex, the medial prefrontal cortex, the mammillary body of the hypothalamus and the lateral septal area.

So, highly modified sensory information has already formed a network before reaching the entorhinal cortex and hippocampus. The tagged neurons within this network could form the basis of a memory engram that is already distributed. The only thing hippocampal regions would have to do is to strengthen this engram network during LTP and consolidation, and then periodically stimulate it with LTD.

Initial LTP produces no genetic changes, but during prolonged LTP, signalling cascades within the cell could activate protein synthesis. This could modify the nature and strength of the synaptic connections that have been formed. Once these have strengthened and consolidated enough, it would only need the intermittent stimulation of LTD to maintain the network over a long period. Of course, some of the synaptic connections would deteriorate with time, leading to the patchy recall we are all familiar with. The emotional aspect of the memory may deteriorate the quickest if consolidation mainly occurs within the cortex.

Even though there is logic to it, this explanation may turn out to be too simplistic, partly right or even completely wrong. It is the way science works. At any rate, this fascinating research continues.

So now we have seen some of the ways in which our life experiences can be stored, then recalled when needed, in ways both fast and slow, and how recall of these experiences is not like playing an old movie. What we get recalled is often a skeletonised, chewed-at version of experience, free of shadows and often attached to emotion, but representative and useful enough.

Next up is the wrap, what this book has really been about — the many ways we can interpret our world. Perception they call it, and in the words of the gone-before, that's all there is, my friend.

But logically, this next chapter should perhaps appear before the chapter on memory because, as we have just seen, perception produces a large part of the raw material for memory. But perception also relies on memory to interpret the current information to produce a percept of the world around us. A two-way street. That means our perception of the present can be influenced by what we've experienced before. This also feeds into the argument about whether we really do have freedom of choice in how we think.

6

Perception

Here we are at the end — or is it the beginning? ***Perception* — the P in FACE MaP.**

It is the sum of all the parts before — the wrap. This chapter will deal with how sensation is produced, and how this neural activity can be modified to form a percept, our own personal interpretation, rightly or wrongly, of the world out there.

We have a basic problem with reality: we don't yet know what it is. And there are other questions too, such as: How do we perceive our world and our relationship within it? What is truth? Can the ultimate truth lie only within us and not be related to external truth at all? If so, is there no true external truth? Or is it the other way around? What if the external truth is real and our perception of it false?

We do know that we create our own unified coherent sense of reality, but for now we have to realise that all may not be what it seems — and the science bears this out.

The insightful, existential Jack Kerouac, writing in *The Dharma Bums* and drawing on ideas from Goethe to Sartre, sums up perception perfectly:

> *Your mind makes out the orange by seeing it, hearing it, touching it, smelling it, tasting it and thinking about it but without this mind, you call it, the orange would not have been seen or heard or smelled or tasted or even mentally noticed, it's actually, that orange, depending on your mind to exist! Don't you see that? By itself it's a no-thing, it's really mental, it's seen only of your mind.*

The Irish philosopher George Berkeley also thought about the issue. He asked the well-known question: If a tree falls in the forest, and no one hears it, does it make a sound? Does the answer have to be 'No'?

We do know that our own reality is formed by how we see the world outside and by how we see ourselves, our sense of self. This mix of what we see and what we feel forms a conscious perception of where we are in the moment, a *percept*. And this percept could form the basis of memory, the engram. And how this engram relates to our inner narrative is another interesting question. Does our internal narrative drive perception?

The process of perception combines the powers of the frontal cortex and associated attention and consciousness and working-memory, along with emotion and long-term memory, into this one phantasmagorical dish labelled a percept. Reflecting the universe it has to understand, the process of perception is multilayered, hierarchical and influenced from the bottom up and from the top down. Forward-driving incoming sensations can influence how we think from the bottom up, and cognition using memory and emotion can influence, in a top-down way, our interpretation of incoming sensations, either directly or by modulation.

We can receive pressure waves of different frequencies travelling through air or water but we hear them as words or music or noise. We can receive electromagnetic waves of different frequencies, but we see them as colours. As Kerouac says, these sounds or visions are mental creations produced by the cognitive processes that follow a sensory experience and don't exist outside the brain.

We have the five main 'perceptual abilities of seeing, hearing, smelling, tasting and touching'. There are also other 'perceptual abilities' related to pain and body position, and that important sixth sense of intuition. These are 'analytical triumphs' enabling us to rapidly analyse the sights and sounds and smells of faces and voices to see what they are telling us (Kandel, 2013). But do we always see what we think we see? Maybe not.

How perception drives behaviour has been succinctly described by Conway and Rehding (2013). Modified signals from receptors, such as those in the retina of the eye or the basilar membrane of the ear, are eventually processed in a series of regions in the cerebral cortex to 'compute descriptions of the world: what or where objects are'. Signals are then sent from these cortical areas to other brain structures, such as the anterior cingulate cortex, that evaluate choices and compare rewards. This attaches meaning to the sensory descriptions. Eventually, 'guided by learning, memory, and emotions', decisions are made.

Mathematical models and probability

Ideas around perception have been part of the psychological study of judgement since the mid-1950s. The lens model produced by Brunswik in 1955, compares the analysis of the judge with what the diagnosis is. This analysis or perception of the judge is made by examining a set of cues, such as symptoms and signs. The difference between the judge's analysis and the diagnosis is a measurement of the clinician's accuracy and can be measured many times, over different scenarios, to give an average hit rate.

For example, a clinician examining a patient would take a history and perform an examination. If the symptom was headache, finding out the blood pressure of the patient could lead to the clinician making a judgement concerning the patient's diagnosis, such as hypertension or tension headache or even worse, an intracranial bleed. In this model, 'judgements are made on tangible data which serve as cues to intangible events' (Elstein and Bordage, 1998).

In real life, clinicians do this all the time. No patient comes in with a label on their forehead saying: 'I've got Z wrong with me'. That's why they have come to a clinician, whose expertise can hopefully sort things out. Clinicians are constantly using data from what they see or hear or feel, to try and work out what's wrong with the patient.

And we do this in our personal lives all the time as well. We might see our friends or neighbours arguing and try to understand 'Why?' We might try to understand and therefore hopefully predict the movements on the stock market or the price of oil.

Mathematical concepts have long been used to help in our understanding of the world and our prediction of the future. One important concept is *cue weighting*: how strong is the relationship between the cue, such as headache or blood pressure, and the diagnosis, such as hypertension, tension headache or an intracerebral bleed. A cue with a strong relationship with the diagnosis will be more useful than a cue with a weak relationship.

To decide what a cue is has a perceptive quality. Why do we choose to use only some elements out of the big picture before us? How do we determine what packet of information is useful to us now in this context? And once chosen, how relevant is the cue to solving the problem? Cue weighting is one concept that helps in this.

Probability

Cue weighting is usually subjective but can be objectively measured using *probability*: what is the probability that this headache, in this situation, means an intracranial bleed is taking place?

The idea that we are all 'naive intuitive statisticians' and that improving our statistical abilities could influence how we think, has persisted since the time of Brunswik — despite experienced clinicians reporting that they make use of patterns not statistics. Current neuroscience would suggest that when time is short and the clinician is experienced in the domain, (s)he is right. But evidence from psychology also suggests that once the tools of probability are learned, they can be very useful. Unfortunately, this evidence also shows that our own judgement of probability, our *subjective probability*, is often wrong. The phenomenon of 'bootstrapping' is where algorithms outperform humans. This happens in most domains (Connolly et al., 2000).

It is not easy to use probability accurately. Firstly, the underlying concepts need to be learned. Then the information used to calculate probabilities needs to be reviewed constantly and monitored for accuracy, as it may change. Algorithms should never be static if used in medicine. But in the right context and with the right information, probability can be useful. 'Opportunities may be lost if the doctor does not know how to use this informal normative reasoning tool' (Hamm, 1988).

So, what is probability? Basically, it is the likelihood of an event happening. It is the percentage chance of an event happening within a sample space, expressed as a number between zero and one. We use phrases such as: there is a probability of 0.7 that event A will happen, given certain conditions. We can also use the term 'risk' when we talk about probabilities, but we use percentages when describing it: there is a 70% risk of event A happening, given certain conditions (Durrrett, 1994).

Conditional probability is more commonly used in medicine and in discussions around memory recall and perception. It can be defined as the likelihood that something is true given a piece of information: if event A happens, what is the likelihood that event B will happen? It is all about interpreting what we see, realising that the information is limited, and trying to find the truth or predict the future. What can I infer from this information? What is the likelihood that what I see before me really does mean this or that is going to happen? What is this person really like based on what I can see? We try and evaluate the probability of uncertain events happening so we can then make decisions about what to do.

The original theorem describing conditional probability is Bayes' theorem. It is an equation about conditional probability, where the probability of an event occurring is conditional on the probability of *another* related event.

In medicine, it is used in situations where we need to know what the probability of diagnosis is when we receive a test result. If event A is a test result, we can then use this to determine the probability that event B, the diagnosis, has occurred.

Bayes' theorem can be used to calculate post-test probabilities (or odds) based on pretest probabilities and the sensitivity and specificity of a test. Sensitivity is a measure of how many people who truly have the disease will test positive, and specificity is a measure of how many people who don't have the disease will test negative. These are measures of how effective a symptom, or sign, or test is in identifying a disease and in discriminating between it and other diseases or an otherwise normal state of health.

Sensitivities and specificities are not constants for a particular event. They are context specific. A good example is urine testing for pregnancy. It is not until two to three weeks after conception, or four to five weeks after the last period, that most urine tests become positive in a normal pregnancy. So the test has different sensitivity and specificity depending on the test used and the stage of the pregnancy.

Models of inference using Bayesian techniques are used in perception, as we shall see (Powers et al., 2017). There is more on probability in the section on Definitions.

Other models

Two other thinking processes related to perception are *induction* and *deduction*. All of us use these in our daily lives.

Induction is where a perceived package of information, such as a stimulus or a cue or an event, induces in us an explanation for that event. It is similar to the rapid emotional processing of information in intuition. Induction moves from the particular to the general: What does that information in this context actually mean? Why did this happen now? Can a rule be applied?

Induction is influenced by expectations that come from our knowledge and beliefs based on previous experience and current context. These expectations have been called 'priors' (Powers et al., 2017). For example, if we see someone on the street, we immediately form a perception of them based on a few defining traits, such as race or class. We form a prior expectation of what this person is based on what we think of the group they belong to. This meshes our beliefs about the other with current context, including culture and examples that easily spring to mind, or 'availability', as Tversky and Kahneman called it. This rapid perception is similar to the intuitive judging of things as 'good' or 'bad', as discussed in the section on emotion.

Deduction is where an explanation for what is happening is then tested to reinforce or refute the explanation, moving from the general to the particular. Mainstream media tend to use a deductive process, generally coming from an established point of view and selecting examples which reinforce that point of view. One of the classic theories around medical decision-making suggests that clinicians are induced by the events before them to produce hypotheses about the true cause of these events. From these broad hypotheses they can then deduce, after searching for further evidence, which hypothesis is right or wrong. This process has been called a 'hypothetico-deductive' approach (Elstein et al., 1978).

Two other words need explanation: inference and implication.

Inference is a passive process where we draw conclusions about what something is when we don't know much about it, such as looking at a painting or a sculpture. It is a passive action that can happen rapidly, like intuition. The direction of the process is inwards, towards us.

Implication on the other hand, is an active process where we will actively suggest what something is, or what will happen in a particular situation. The direction of the process is outwards.

How a percept is produced

So how do we interpret the many millions of pieces of sensory information coming at us every second? The process of perception does it. It translates a complex environment into something useful that we can relate to and understand — the percept. The physical properties of the stimulus are converted into neural activity, which is modified and transformed over a series of steps from the periphery, through to the spinal cord and then into the brain where the final percept is produced. A lot of information is lost in the process.

Our bodies are covered in a wide array of sensory receptors that code for physical properties such as light, heat, chemicals and touch. Each receptor acts as a filter for a narrow, optimal range of values for a stimulus. It is tuned to that stimulus if it activates the receptor at low energy and produces the strongest response. These responses translate the physical analogue properties of the stimulus into digital electrical activity, which is centrally propagated along sensory neurons to produce what we feel (Kandel, 2013). This coded digital representation of information passes through various relay stations, including ganglia outside the spine and areas of grey matter within the dorsal horn of the spinal cord. Information coming in is transformed within the relay stations and then these changed packages of information are transmitted up the spinal cord into the brain stem.

Modification occurs at the receptor level, from other sensory neurons, within the spinal cord and in higher centres. For example, if a stimulus is constant, the receptor can adapt and we no longer feel the stimulus; it has faded from our consciousness, habituated. And there are rapid- and slow-adapting receptors.

Within each relay station, such as the dorsal ganglia or the dorsal horn, each incoming sensory neurone has excitatory neurones converging on it in the presynaptic pathway. This can lead to the stimulation of many postsynaptic neurons. Each class of sensory neuron makes connections with specific separate groups of central neurons, producing sensory systems that terminate in brain regions specifically designated for cognition and action. The systems are multilayered, hierarchical and influenced from the bottom up and from the top down. Forward-driving sensory inputs are not just 'passively received'. They influence perception from the bottom up (Kandel, 2013).

Perception is also influenced in a top-down way by higher level cognition using memory and emotion. We actively infer what causes the sensations we feel 'from expectations based on memories gained from previous experience, or priors'. These prior expectations and inputs can be combined using Bayes' theorem in some mathematical models. 'In these models the mismatch that can occur between priors and inputs is called the prediction error and could theoretically be used to update belief systems' (Powers et al., 2017).

In another article using similar modelling, in 2017, Krishnamurthy and his colleagues suggested 'prior expectations can be used to improve perceptual judgements about ambiguous stimuli'.

The next sections will now show how we see, appreciate beauty and music, feel the pain and imagine the placebo before being framed, as we finally conclude with a simple story for you to read.

How we see — vision as a model of perception

Perception is about combining all the features about an object, image, place or thing, into a single unified whole — the percept. It is similar to the unified, subjective, qualitative whole of consciousness. It is not about interpreting every single stimulus we come in contact with. Perceptual unity is eventually achieved by a distributed network in the brain, where information is processed in many areas that are fed by at least two parallel interacting pathways.

How we see is a good example of how perception works. The physical stimulus of light is initially converted into a series of neural impulses or signals. These are then further modified through a series of steps until an interpretation is formed that appears in our mind's eye — the percept. Vision is not simply a reconstruction like a photograph. In a photograph, coloured dots of point-to-point light intensities coalesce to form the image.

Light is a form of electromagnetic radiation (EM radiation) and can be produced from a variety of sources. The primary properties of EM radiation are intensity, direction of movement or propagation, frequency or wavelength spectrum, and polarisation. Light visible to us has a range or spectrum of wavelengths of around 400 nm for ultraviolet light, up to 700 nm for infrared light. There is much more on the physical nature of light in the Definitions section in Part Two.

This visible light is converted into neural impulses, and the conversion begins in the retina at the back of the eye. All our visual experience relies on this neural membrane. The modified output from this 'window on the world' is transmitted to the brain by one million optic nerve fibres, but nearly half the cerebral cortex is used to process this output. Visual information that is lost in the retina 'can never be recovered'.

The retina is a 'thin sheet of neurons, a few hundred micrometres thick that wraps around inside the back of the eye from the iris backwards. The photoreceptor cells in the outermost layer absorb light and convert it to a neural signal by phototransduction (Kandel, 2013).

Light is transformed into neural signals in receptor cells using a form of vitamin A called retinal. This is present at the tip of the receptor and changes shape when struck by photons of light. This change in shape starts a series of chemical reactions that are converted into neural signals, which are eventually conveyed along the optic nerve to be interpreted by the brain.

There are two types of receptor cells in the retina — rods and cones — and each type acts as a filter for a narrow range of bandwidth. Rods work well in dim light and occur mainly on the periphery of the retina, increasing our peripheral vision in the dark. Cones are concentrated around the centre of the back of the retina in an area called the fovea.

A few millimetres outside the fovea, rods outnumber cones, and all photoreceptors become larger and more widely spaced towards the periphery. Impulses from many rods connect to a single ganglion. This is stimulated only when enough impulses have arrived, and acts as an efficient filter. Rods are extremely sensitive to light and can pick up a single photon, but as the level of light increases, the rods respond less to variations in intensity (Kandel, 2013).

There are three types of cones, and each has a particular sensitivity to a certain band of visible light:

- The S, short-wavelength, or blue, cones
- The M, medium-wavelength, or green, cones
- The L, long-wavelength, or red, cones.

There is a graded photosensitivity in these receptors, enabling us to perceive a wide range of colours through varying combinations of photoreceptors.

For instance, at the preferred wavelength of the green cones, the blue cones don't respond at all, and the red cones respond only very weakly, assisting the eye to 'see' the colour green. At a wavelength in the orange part of the spectrum, blue cones are not activated, green cones respond weakly and red cones are activated strongly, enabling us to 'see' the combination of red and green that is orange.

Generally only one cone connects with one ganglion cell and because they are concentrated around the fovea, our central vision is crisper and clearer and less ambiguous, and loaded towards seeing in daylight. At night-time the central fovea is blind due to the absence of rods. To see something at night, we must look to one side of the object, a fact that astronomers know well when looking at the stars. If an object is focused on in poor light, it disappears and then returns in our peripheral vision when we look away (Kandel, 2013).

As well as the vertical pathway between the outer layers of the retina and the ganglion cells, there are 'many lateral connections provided by the horizontal cells in the outer synaptic layer and the amacrine cells in the inner synaptic layer'. This helps the retinal circuit to perform low-level visual processing, extracting 'from the raw images in the left and right eyes certain spatial and temporal features'.

This is the initial stage in the analysis of visual images as the retina adjusts its sensitivity to the 'ever-changing conditions of illumination' to produce perceptual constancy. For instance, we might be talking to a friend on the deck outside in the bright light of a ski field on a sunny day then both go inside to get some food. Even though there has been a sudden change in the conditions of illumination inside, we will still recognise the colour of the jacket our friend is wearing (Kandel, 2013). There is more detail about the retina in Brain Biology and the Glossary in Part Two.

Retinal ganglion cells are the output neurons from the retina and form the optic nerve. Impulses pass along the optic nerve from the back of the eye to the lateral geniculate nucleus of the thalamus where they are processed before being passed on to the visual cortex in the occipital lobe and to the visual association areas of the cortex for further processing. Some information is discarded by the thalamus, and some information is added in the association areas to produce what we 'see' as the 'picture' before us. There is more detailed information about the structure and function of the thalamus in Brain Biology and the Glossary in Part Two.

Once visual information has been processed in the thalamus and has arrived at the primary visual cortex, it is divided into what needs to be acted on immediately and what is needed to identify the content, location and movement of the images. Information about the content of an image is conveyed by a ventral pathway to areas in the temporal cortex and from there to the prefrontal cortex and also to areas involved with memory, the hippocampus and entorhinal cortex. Areas in the parietal lobe analyse information about location and movement that is then transferred by a dorsal pathway to motor areas of the frontal cortex controlling movements of the eyes, arms and hands. This is how we use vision to guide our own movements.

To get the final image that we 'see', a visual scene is broken down into its components and analysed within the brain at three different levels of complexity — low, intermediate and high.

- At the lowest level, different features within the scene, such as local contrast, orientation, colour and movement, are singled out.

- At the intermediate level, the arrangement of scenes and surface properties are analysed. The visual image of the scene is overlaid onto surfaces and their contours, and the foreground is singled out from the background.
- At the highest level, the objects within the scene are recognised, then 'the objects can be matched with memories of shapes and their associated meanings' (Kandel, 2013).

The analysis of the visual scene is a constructive process that obeys simple rules, first developed by the German psychologists Max Wertheimer, Kurt Koffka and Wolfgang Köhler from the ideas of Immanuel Kant.

They formed the school of Gestalt psychology in the late nineteenth century. They argued that 'the brain has a way of looking at the world, a set of expectations that derives in part from experience and in part from built-in neural wiring'. They described three simple laws of visual perception:

- Similarity
- Proximity
- Good continuation. This is important for merging linear elements into unified shapes with smooth boundaries that become obvious and 'pop out from complex backgrounds'.

The remaining laws of visual perception that were described later are:

- Separation of the object from the background
- Segmentation.

Segmentation of the objects in the visual field relies not just on geometric principles, but also on attention and expectation. Context influences perception; wherever we are, we know what to expect. This expectation bias primes us to merge all the visual elements of the scene before us into one 'unified percept' and helps produce 'a perceptual constancy' (Kandel, 2013).

Expectation may be due to the brain using patterns that are memories of shapes and their associated meanings. Experts use patterns more than novices within a particular domain. It is a fast method of interpreting information in a rapidly changing and potentially dangerous world. We want to know quickly whether there is a threat in the scene before us, and we can all read faces quickly.

So, can you read this?

7H15 M3554G3 53RV35 70 PR0V3 H0W 0UR M1NDS C4N D0 4M4Z1NG 7H1NGS! 1MPRE331V3 7H1NG5! 1N 7H3 B3G1NN1NG 17 WA5 H4RD BU7 N0W, Y0UR MIND 1S R34D1NG 17 4U70M471C4LLY W17H 0U7 3V3N 7H1NK1NG 4B0U7 17!

And this?

Can you raed this? Olny 55 plepoe out of 100 can. I cdnuolt blveiee that I cluod aulaclty uesdnatnrd what I was rdanieg. The phaonmneal pweor of the human mind. Aoccdrnig to rseearch at Cmabrigde Uinervtisy, it dseno't mtater in what oerdr the ltters in a word are, the only iproamtnt tihng is that the frsit and last ltteers be in the rghit pclae.

After the initial confusion has worn off, these examples are easy to read. We have learned the rules. The important rules we need to know in order to understand the second example are that all the letters in each word need to be there and that the first and last letters of each word are in the right place. This last rule also explains why texting works so well.

We see things based on patterns that we know from experience have a relationship to external truth. And if these patterns make up a unified whole that we are comfortable with, that sits well with our emotions, we feel good. But if what we see does not conform to the expected patterns, what happens? We feel uncomfortable. Psychologists have termed this 'cognitive dissonance', produced by various cognitive illusions. The drawings of Escher are a good example. At first glance, the drawings appear real, but our perception and emotions tell us that all is not quite right, and when we look closer we can see why.

Visual illusions — mistakes that 'seeing' makes

A visual percept is not necessarily a true representation of external reality. The laws of visual perception described above contribute to some well-known visual illusions. These illusions are constant, unlike the 'illusions' of magic that disappear when we have figured out the deception.

A typical visual illusion is that of the full moon coming up over the eastern horizon. It looks bigger on the horizon than when it's seen a few hours later at its zenith in the sky. We normally judge the proximity of objects like the moon by comparing them with features in the landscape, such as the horizon. The expectation is that objects nearer the horizon are closer and they therefore appear to be larger. So, when the moon is rising, there is no separation from the horizon and it appears larger. When it's high in the sky it is surrounded by sky and stars and clouds, we perceive it to be farther away and hence it appears smaller.

There are many other illusions in nature. When we are on a snowy mountain slope on a dull day, or on a boat on a featureless ocean, it is hard to gauge distance because of the lack of continuity, separation and segmentation.

When we look into the distance, things that are clearer will seem closer to us, and things that are blurred will seem further away. If we also rely on this rule in other situations, it can lead to error.

When driving on a grey, misty day or at sunset, distance is deceptive. Because of the lack of detail in the low light, other cars on the road appear further away than they actually are. This increases the risk of oncoming traffic overtaking or turning off the road in front of us. Think 'James Dean in his Porsche Spyder'. We can reduce this risk by turning our headlights on. This won't just make it easier for oncoming motorists to see us, but the brightness of the lights will also make *us* seem closer, reducing the risk to us.

If we look at an evenly spaced six-by-six pattern of two different types of dots on a page, we see a pattern of alternating rows if the dots in each row are similar. If the dots in the columns are similar, we see an alternating pattern of columns. If the dots in the pattern are all the same but those in the columns are arranged closer together than those in the rows, we see them arranged in columns. These illusions can be explained by the 'expectation bias' (Kandel, 2013).

There are many other examples of visual illusions that can be explained by the expectation bias. The Penrose Stairs was created by Lionel Penrose after his son was introduced to Escher's work at a conference in Rome in 1954. They show a set of steps arranged in the shape of a square that appear to continually ascend, despite looking impossible. The steps form a paradoxical illusion dependent on a cognitive expectation that adjacent edges must join.

These cognitive expectations are basically our visual assumptions about the world, largely based on patterns stored in both episodic and semantic memory. These assumptions produce subconscious inferences, an idea first suggested by Hermann Helmholtz in the nineteenth century. These subconscious inferences are also produced when we are primed, as we have seen in the section on implicit memory.

There are many other types of visual illusions related to cognitive processes — distorting illusions, ambiguous illusions and the fictional illusions of schizophrenics or those taking hallucinogens. Distorting illusions have distortions of size, length or curvature, such as the Müller-Lyer illusion or the café wall illusion. Ambiguous illusions are generated when there are alternative perceptual explanations for the same object, such as the Rubin vase or the Necker cube (see www.unisaustralia.com, search for Cognitive Illusions).

How we see colour

Like sound, light is made of waves of different frequencies transmitted through a medium such as air or water. As Newton said, light is essentially colourless. Light waves hit the retina and are then processed into what we call colour. Colour and its associations become deeply ingrained within us. Red is the colour of life, of the blood within us, and when it drains away, our life drains with it and we turn a pale, blue or purple hue. These are the colours associated with cold and lifelessness. Red is also the colour of rage or anger, of the flush of sexual arousal or the blush of embarrassment.

There is a vast literature on how colour can influence how we think. From marketing to sexual attraction to athletic prowess, the effects of colour seem to be everywhere. But research has been dogged by methodological problems in the definition and measurement of colour and in the design of the experiments. The effects appear to depend to a large extent on cultural interpretations.

Some experiments have shown that men tend to interpret red clothing on a woman as a sexual signal. Others show that women may perceive a man in red to be of higher status, which can affect how they rate his attractiveness and sexual desirability. Some have shown that viewing red can reduce performance on complicated tasks requiring verbal reasoning, working-memory and creativity, while others have shown that viewing red improves performance on simpler tasks. Or that blue or green may be useful for creative performance and yellow may be detrimental in some challenging cognitive tasks (Elliot et al., 2014).

But seeing colour is not a result of a simple transference of colour-related information from the retina to the brain. Otherwise we would see the same object in a variety of colours, depending on the illumination of that object. When we come in from the glaring sun of a snowfield into a darker room, the colour of our jacket stays the same, even though the light coming onto the retina is vastly different in the two situations. Similarly, if we watch a person going away from us, we judge that person's size to be the same.

This shows that the basic principles of scene analysis by the visual system in the brain construct stable representations from this brief and 'variable stimulation of the retina'. If we based vision only on the analysis of the physical qualities of the object at the time, the colours we see would change. So, light arriving on different parts of the retina is compared in context so it can calculate the physical qualities of the surface of the object (Kandel, 2013).

Now we'll look at how perception is actively involved in creativity and art, and passively involved in how we see beauty and attractiveness.

Creating art, admiring beauty and attractiveness

What is art?

That is a question to which the answer is elusive, but once again the frontal cortex, particularly the lateral prefrontal cortex, may play a pivotal role. Creativity is an active process. Some would say it is the pinnacle of flexible thinking. Underlying our creativity is an ability to break with convention and previous patterns of thinking, to think conceptually and abstractly, and to adopt new rules.

As we have seen, knowledge and memory are stored in a distributed network within the temporal, occipital and parietal cortical areas (TOP). New forms of that knowledge are produced by areas in the prefrontal cortex, particularly the DLPFC, using working-memory. This is important in 'understanding the relationship between knowledge and creativity, as well as the difference between creative and non-creative thinking'. Creativity needs the cognitive abilities of working-memory, sustained attention, cognitive flexibility and judgement of propriety. The prefrontal cortex has all of these abilities (Dietrich, 2004).

So then, what is art? Once an object such as a painting has been created, why is one object seen as art and another not? What makes an object, thing or place beautiful? Why do we find some people attractive?

The question of 'What is art?' has no doubt been debated since people first made handprints and drawings on the roofs and walls of caves, or drawings in the sand with a stick. It is bound with creativity, the artist and reward: we have to connect with the object, place or person, a process that usually involves emotion and reward.

The common threads in all these questions are perception and context. Once an object has been created, it must then be perceived as a work of art. The features of the object have to be perceived by others, interpreted and then an answer found, a decision made. It is an internal process, dependent on belief and previous experience, and influenced by our external context, particularly culture.

In the preface to his only novel *The Picture of Dorian Gray* published in 1891, that great, vilified, late-nineteenth-century playwright Oscar Wilde, discusses the relationship between art and beauty somewhat whimsically, and certainly with an arrogance common to Europeans of his social status at that time. Read through a twenty-first-century lens, it makes interesting reading:

> *The artist is the creator of beautiful things*
>
> *To reveal art and conceal the artist is art's aim ...*
>
> *Those who find ugly meanings in beautiful things are corrupt without being charming. This is a fault.*
>
> *Those who find beautiful meanings in beautiful things are the cultivated. For these there is hope ...*
>
> *The moral life of man forms part of the subject matter of the artist, but the morality of art consists in the perfect use of an imperfect medium.*
>
> *No artist desires to prove anything. Even things that are true can be proved ...*
>
> *All art is at once surface and symbol.*
>
> *Those who go beneath the surface do so at their peril.*
>
> *Those who read the symbol do so at their peril.*
>
> *It is the spectator, and not life, that art really mirrors ...*

There is plenty there to think about and only part of the preface has been quoted, but it illustrates one of the functions of art: to provoke discussion. It also illustrates another important concept: thinking cohabits with context. What has been said in a past context may not be appropriate in a different, later context.

Beauty and attractiveness

Beauty and attractiveness are defined in slightly different ways. Beauty is more in the eye of the beholder, the individual, varying from person to person and having an emotional element. If an object, place or person is deemed beautiful, it means there has been perception and reward. It is a much more active process.

But within philosophy and art, there is no agreement on what is the nature of beauty. The English Romantic poet John Keats, in the last two lines of his 'Ode on a Grecian Urn' written in May 1819, the year he contracted tuberculosis, writes of beauty:

> *Beauty is truth, truth beauty — that is all*
> *Ye know on earth, and all ye need to know*

Immanuel Kant thought we could only see beauty if we were in a state of 'disinterested contemplation'. Friedrich Nietzsche thought beauty involved sensual attraction, and the French novelist Stendhal defined beauty as the 'promise of happiness'. None of these views are universally accepted because the definition of what is beautiful depends on context. Beauty has different functions within different societies, and within different philosophical points of view, and is sometimes seen in connection with epistemology or ethics (Conway and Rehding, 2013).

A common belief is that beauty is a constant, with rules that define it. But beauty, as in most perceptual responses, 'is an analogue, not binary, condition that varies in complex ways with exposure, context, attention and rest'. It is likely that this depends on 'activity across many distributed brain regions —

specifically those responsible for perception, reward, decision-making and emotion' (Conway and Rehding, 2013).

Beauty then can be seen only through the eye of the beholder, depends on context and is associated with a sense of wonder and uniqueness.

Attractiveness though, is a more culturally uniform percept. It is a descriptor, devoid of emotion. To say something is attractive is much more intuitive than saying something is beautiful. Attractiveness is to intuition or fast thinking as beauty is to analysis or slow thinking.

Attractiveness just is. It doesn't need to be thought about. Unlike beauty, it draws no sudden intake of breath, no unspoken 'wow', it just is. Even when it is spoken out loud, the word 'attractive' is bland, succinct and unobtrusive, whereas the word 'beautiful' is spoken with a richness and lilt that conjures up allure, excitement and passion, indicating the evocative power of language.

We all have different ideas about what is beautiful, but there is some agreement on what is found to be attractive. We can all agree that some people just stand out from the crowd. Attractiveness can be seen as subtly different, distinct, innate and measurable. Many different factors have been studied, including facial and body symmetry, the golden ratio, reduction in oxidative stress, outgoing personality, ratio of torso to leg length, and waist hip ratio amongst others, but with no overall agreement. So attractive people are, just, well, attractive, which shows that the percept of 'attractiveness' may rely more on cultural context than measurement (Conway and Rehding, 2013).

Interestingly though, attractive faces are seen as socially rewarding. Studies using fMRI have shown that viewing attractive faces activates the nucleus accumbens, the orbitofrontal cortex and the ventral striatum, which are all part of the reward system (Quingguo, 2015).

There is no doubt that attractive people fare better in life in general. They are their own reward, and just being around attractive people is rewarding to others. The halo effect is where first impressions influence perception, where one trait, such as attractiveness, influences our perception of what that person is really like.

In one study, Solomon Asch presented descriptions of two people and asked for comments on their personality:

- Alan — intelligent, industrious, impulsive, critical, stubborn, envious
- Ben — envious, stubborn, critical, impulsive, industrious, intelligent.

Looking closely, we can see that the list of descriptions for Alan, are the reverse of the list for Ben, but most people favoured Alan. So, sequence of presentation matters, because in our instinctive attempts to achieve emotional coherence 'the halo effect increases the weight of first impressions' (Kahneman, 2011).

This is just as we have seen in the tests of IFR and ISR, mentioned in the chapter on short-term memory, where items presented first were amongst the most recalled. The halo effect is also well known in the field of politics, where candidates rated 'attractive' do better than those rated less attractive (Todorov,

2009). It just goes to show that a little superficial knowledge about someone can truly be a dangerous thing.

The role of attractiveness has been studied in many different domains. In strategic games, attractive faces can be perceived as 'evolutionarily valuable'. In evolutionary theory, people with attractive faces are thought to be healthier, more fertile and live longer. Workers of above-average beauty are more likely to be hired and promoted and earn ten to fifteen per cent more than workers of below-average beauty. This has been labelled the 'theory of beauty premium and plain penalty' (Quingguo, 2015).

A large meta-analysis of attractiveness bias showed that 'physical attractiveness is always an asset' — regardless of the sex of the candidate, the type of tasks for which the candidates were considered, or how much work experience and job-relevant information the candidate had (Hosoda et al., 2003).

There is no doubt that attractive people fare better in many aspects of life, including work. Attractiveness bias, where people are treated differently depending on their physical appearance, is pervasive in the workplace. In job selection, attractive candidates are generally preferred to those who are equally qualified but unattractive. This bias is common in selection decisions, because in these situations decision-makers generally encounter candidates for the first time. Because of the halo effect described above, these initial impressions of attractiveness have the greatest effect on how the candidate is perceived (Lee et al., 2013).

This can be a problem. Selection decisions based on criteria unrelated to work performance can lead to suboptimal staffing outcomes that can threaten the success of an organisation. This is also important for social equity, because selection decisions are one of the most important factors in career success.

But attractiveness can also have its downside. Sunyoung Lee and his colleagues used various social theories, such as status generalisation theory and interdependence theory, to try and understand how hirers decide who to select for a job, and how they use attractiveness bias. Using status generalisation theory, they suggest that hirers link the attractiveness of candidates to competence in men but not in women. They then use interdependence theory to suggest that attractiveness bias can be used differently by hirers, depending on whether the hirers expect to co-operate or compete with the candidates they are hiring.

When the hirers expect to *co-operate* with the candidate, they perceive attractive male candidates to be more capable co-operators and are biased *towards* them. When the hirers expect to *compete* with the candidate, they perceive attractive male candidates to be more capable competitors and are biased *against* them. In evolutionary terms, it may be that attractive same-sex candidates are seen as a greater threat to the hirer's mating opportunities. So society in general is biased towards attractive people, but when there is a possibility of competition in the organisation in the future, they can be discriminated against if they are being hired by someone of the same sex (Lee et al., 2013).

The sounds of music

Sound consists of waves of alternating increasing and decreasing pressure, transmitted through a medium, such as air or water, with changing amplitude and frequency. The height, or amplitude, of these waves gives sound its loudness, its energy and its intensity. A large wave crashing on the beach sounds louder and has more energy than a small wave. We hear an equal increment in loudness for around every tenfold increase in sound intensity, so a logarithmic scale is used to measure loudness in decibels (dB). The loudest sound we can tolerate is around 120 dB, but this only increases the local atmospheric pressure by a tiny ±0.1%. The frequency of the sound waves the human ear can most effectively hear is between around 1 and 4 kHz, or 1,000 to 4,000 cycles per second.

Hearing is produced when these sound waves are focused by the auricle of the ear into the ear canal, causing the eardrum at the end to vibrate. Within the middle ear cavity, behind the eardrum, there are three small bones, called ossicles, lined up in a row: the malleus, the incus and the stapes. The malleus is inserted into the eardrum and the stapes inserted into the oval window, which is an opening in the cochlea, the organ where sound is converted into nerve impulses. When the eardrum vibrates and moves the ossicles, the stapes acts like a piston, producing pressure waves within the cochlea.

Externally, the cochlea is a coiled structure like a nautilus shell, deep within the temporal bone of the lateral skull, measuring around nine millimetres across — the size of a chickpea. There are three fluid-filled cavities running the length of the cochlea separated by two membranes, the basilar membrane and the tectorial membrane. The 'organ of Corti' lies on the basilar membrane and has three lines of outer hair cells and one line of inner hair cells, each with protruding stereocilia, or tiny hairs. There are around 16,000 of these cells in each cochlea.

The three rows of outer hair cells are attached to the tectorial membrane above, whereas the inner hair cells aren't and move freely within the salty endolymph. Pressure waves within the cochlea produce movements of the basilar membrane, affecting movements of the stereocilia which are then converted into neural impulses.

The outer hair cells probably produce amplification of the atomic level changes in pressure, and have inputs from the superior olivary complex in the pons and a small output to the cochlear nuclei in the medulla of the brain stem. The inner hair cells are responsible for most of the information used in hearing.

The movement of the basilar membrane depends on the frequency of the sound. High-frequency sounds produce maximal movement of the basilar membrane near the oval window, whereas low-frequency sounds produce maximal movement towards the tip of the basilar membrane. Because of this, hair cells are tuned to a certain frequency.

The information from the inner hair cells is conveyed by the cochlear nerve to the cochlear nuclei in the medulla of the brain stem. From here, information is relayed in parallel to several different target nuclei in the brain stem, eventually ending up in the medial geniculate nucleus of the thalamus before being relayed to the auditory cortex.

Most of the target nuclei in the brain stem receive inputs from both ears. Thus the mechanical energy of the sound waves has been converted to neural impulses, eventually producing an interpretation we can understand. And as in other sensory pathways, there is modulation within the cochlea by nerve impulses from brain stem nuclei, and by the arrangement of hair cell sensory neurons.

As with vision, the brain hears by rapidly analysing small segments of the total sound exposure and matches these segments with examples from memory to create a unified whole, or percept, similar to the way impulses related to touch and pain are converted into a percept. Like interpreting colour in different settings, expectation plays a large part.

And like vision, hearing can make mistakes. It can misinterpret information. Ever been out walking and heard the babbling of the brook or the whisperings of the wind in the trees or the scrambled chatter of waves gently breaking on the shore? In these situations, if you shut your eyes and concentrate, it really can sound as if that brook or those waves are people talking.

Music though is not just sound, it is something different again. It has been described by the French-born composer Edgard Varèse as 'organised noises'. We hear sound, but we can perceive sounds to be either noise or music.

In his entertaining and informative book on music and the brain, *This is Your Brain on Music — The Science of a Human Obsession* published in 2006, Daniel Levitin defines the fundamental, confusing, properties of music:

1. *Pitch.* This is a pure cognitive construct. Pitch is a percept, existing only in our minds, like the colour of Kerouac's orange, or the march of time. It is related to the frequency at which air molecules are vibrating, called the tone, and the relative position of the tone in the musical scale. Each pitch has a name, such as D-flat.

When written down, it is called a note, and a chord has a number of notes. So we hear a tone, but we read a note. They are effectively the same.

2. *Rhythm.* The 'duration of a series of notes', the length of time it takes to play a series of notes and the way these notes 'group together into units'.
3. *Tempo.* The overall speed or pace of the piece of music. It is how fast your body moves when it's in time with the beat.
4. *Contour.* The overall shape of the melody, its topography, how much it goes up and down.
5. *Timbre.* This is a subtler interpretation. It is a kind of 'tonal colour' where individual instruments playing the same note will sound subtly different. Timbre also describes how the same instrument can change its sound as it moves through a range. A trumpet playing a low note will have a warm glow, whereas the same trumpet playing a note at the top of its range will sound like a screech.
6. *Loudness.* This relates, in poorly understood ways, to how much air is displaced when a sound is produced — to the energy an instrument creates — and it could be defined as 'the amplitude of a tone'. It is measured in decibels (dB).
7. *Reverberation.* The size of the room or hall where music is being played, combined with the distance from the source, produces a percept that is often called an echo. This is what separates the sound of singing in the shower from the sound of singing in a concert hall.

The perception of music happens when these seven basic properties can be combined with one another to form 'higher order concepts, such as meter, key, melody and harmony'. Again, a hierarchy exists.

- *Meter* is created by our brains from rhythm and loudness cues. It is defined as how many tones or notes are grouped together per unit of time. Tones are organised into groups of three for a waltz and two or four for a march.
- *Key* relates to 'a hierarchy of importance that exists between tones in a musical piece'. It is a pure human construct.
- *Melody* is the string of tones or chords we pay most attention to. It is the main theme of a piece and the tune we sing along with. Melody has different meanings in different genres of music.
- *Harmony* is about the 'relationship between the pitches of different tones'. It is about what we feel works. The expectations we have may be adhered to or disregarded, boundaries can be pushed. It can be about parallel melodies or a chord progression.

At a neural level, when a chord sounds pleasant or euphonious, nerve signals in the auditory nerve are produced at regular intervals, and the interval between these impulses is related to the period of the pitch. A chord sounds unpleasant or dissonant, when it is not played at a regular interval and it produces irregular firing of the auditory nerve fibres. If the chord or notes are played too close together, they interfere with each other instead of reinforcing each other (Kandel, 2013).

So we can see how vibrating air produces hearing, but the interpretation of sound as music is complex. Again as with most perceptive processes, it is a bottom-up process with the final analysis dependent on some top-down modulation.

Pain hurts

The perception of pain is complex, and many sensory signals may be combined to produce the pain we feel. Pain alerts us to noxious stimuli or injuries that need rapid evasive action or urgent treatment. And pain really does hurt — and when it hurts, we get upset.

We all feel pain differently. As with consciousness, there is a subjectivity to all pain experiences that makes it difficult to study. The same painful stimulus applied to the same person under different circumstances will feel different: nothing is painful to all of us all the time. We hear of the battlefield casualty with terrible injuries who does not feel pain until away from danger in the hospital or first-aid centre, or the injured athlete toughing it out to the end of the game, or the fire dancer skittering across hot embers.

And people who show they are in pain are regarded differently. These are social effects of being in pain. One study investigated social judgements that were made about people who appeared to be in pain. Fifty-six subjects were enrolled in the study, and each viewed two separate video clips of a human figure exercising where only the body motion was visible. The videos were produced by tracking dots placed at various points on the body, like that used in green screen techniques in movie production.

In one of them, the figure showed pain behaviours such as hesitating, holding and rubbing; in the other they didn't. Without any information about the person in each video, the subjects judged each person for characteristics 'associated with interpersonal warmth, competence, mood and physical fitness'.

The person who displayed more pain behaviour was judged 'to be less warm and less competent' than the person who did not appear to be in pain. The mood of the person judged to be in pain was also thought to be more negative, and that person was also judged less fit. There are important implications here for people in chronic pain. These negative evaluations can all affect the social relationships, well-being and pain assessment of these people (Ashton-James et al., 2014).

Feeling pain is the result of a complex perceptive process requiring consciousness and attention, and the level of pain experienced is influenced by context. 'Brave boys don't cry' is a persistent message in the bloody coliseum of school sport. Mood and emotional state also influence pain perception. Pain states can also be divided into acute, prolonged or persistent, and chronic pain.

So what happens when we feel pain?

Pain signals are initially processed peripherally, travelling up the spinal cord in five main pathways, and are then processed centrally. There is a large amount of time overlap, and processing can be going on in several places at the same time.

First, receptors that deal with noxious stimuli are stimulated to produce impulses that travel mainly to the dorsal horn of the spinal cord for the first level of processing. After being processed, the information then ascends in the spinal cord in five separate tracks, with minimal further processing until it reaches the brain stem.

Within the brain stem there are numerous connections with each tract, and further connections to the thalamus and other higher centres, including the cortex. At each stage there are influences from the periphery upward, called bottom-up modulation, and from centrally downward, called top-down modulation.

Perception of pain starts in the periphery. Noxious stimuli arouse specialised sensory receptors called ***nociceptors*** that are widely distributed in many tissues, including skin, bone, joints and muscles. There are three main types of nociceptors: thermal, mechanical and polymodal. These are not specialised receptors like those for touch, but are simply the terminal endings of two types of neurons that convey impulses towards the spinal cord: there are the thinly myelinated Aδ axons that carry impulses at speeds varying between five and thirty metres per second, and the larger non-myelinated C axons that convey impulses at a more leisurely one metre per second.

Thermal nociceptors are activated by temperatures below 5 °C and above 45 °C.

Mechanical nociceptors are activated by intense pressure applied to the skin. Both thermal and mechanical nociceptors are the terminal endings of Aδ axons.

Polymodal nociceptors are activated by high-intensity mechanical, chemical or thermal stimuli and are the endings of C axons.

A class of *silent nociceptors* are found in the internal organs or viscera, activated by inflammation and chemicals that reduce their firing threshold (Kandel, 2013).

Signals from these nociceptors are then conveyed to neurons in the dorsal horn of the spinal cord. The dorsal horn is layered, mimicking the cerebral cortex, each layer receiving different inputs. And, like the cortex, there are a lot of connections between different layers, enabling information processing at the spinal cord level.

Many different sensory modalities that either excite or inhibit with high- or low-threshold inputs converge at spinal or supraspinal sites. It is an efficient set-up for both the perception of pain and the production of rapid automatic activity to reduce how much pain is felt.

For example, if your hand was suddenly hit by a hammer or burnt, one reflex action is to jump up and shake the affected hand to try and reduce the pain. And lo and behold ... it works! Shaking the hand can stimulate large-fibre tracts to suppress the central transmission of the pain signals just generated by the injury, and starved of attention with the effort, the pain just withers away.

And where do we feel the visceral pain that comes from our internal organs? At the dorsal horn there is a cross-connection between fibres coming from these internal organs, like the heart, and those coming from the skin. This leads to what is called referred pain. Heart pain is commonly felt in the left chest, jaw and left arm, whereas gall bladder pain can be felt in the back (Kandel, 2013).

After the nociceptive information has been modified in the dorsal horn, perhaps by passing through a gate-type system, this information then ascends in five major pathways. The largest of these is the ***lateral spinothalamic tract*** which ends at several thalamic nuclei. These thalamic nuclei have connections with areas of the cortex, including the cingulate gyrus and insular cortex of the temporal lobes that contribute to the perception of pain.

Pain signals travelling from the dorsal horn up another pathway, the ***spinomesencephalic tract***, eventually terminate in the amygdala, changing how we feel about the pain.

Information travelling up the ***spinohypothalamic tract*** projects to hypothalamic nuclei, producing the autonomic responses we feel, like sweating and a rapid pulse. Increased cortisol production and adrenalin release occur, which helps us cope with the stress of a painful situation.

There are also descending pathways that affect activity in the dorsal horn, particularly those from the brain stem nuclei of the locus coeruleus, that uses noradrenalin, and the rostral raphe nucleus that uses serotonin.

There are many different types of pain occurring at different stages following exposure to a noxious stimulus. The acute pain that follows when we accidentally hit our thumb with a hammer is felt as a short-lived, sharp, *first pain,* as Aδ fibres carry information from damaged thermal and mechanical receptors. After this we feel a dull *slow pain* transmitted by C axons from polymodal nociceptors that lasts a lot longer, as those of us who have had a battered thumb well know.

Longer-lasting persistent pain can be roughly divided into ***nociceptive pain*** and ***neuropathic pain***.

Nociceptive pain can be caused by changes in nociceptor activity. The inflammation following tissue injury, such as hammering a thumb or spraining an ankle, produces a prolonged release of a mix of chemicals, such as prostaglandins, that continue to activate nociceptors following acute injury. There is also the nociceptive pain from chronic conditions, such as arthritis, or invasion of tissues such as bone by tumour.

The pain of allodynia is when patients feel exaggerated pain in response to a usually benign stimulus, such as a light touch on sunburnt skin, or by gentle movement of small joints in patients with arthritis, or getting out of bed in the morning after a heavy workout. This type of intermittent pain is only felt following a peripheral stimulus. Pain in these conditions would be felt by most people, and is generally classed as normal unless it becomes prolonged.

Then there is the more persistent pain of hyperalgesia. This is an exaggerated response to a normal stimulus produced by a sensitisation of peripheral nociceptors to prostaglandins and can persist without sensory stimulation (Kandel, 2013).

Neuropathic pain is completely different. Here the pain results from direct injury to nerves in the peripheral or central nervous system, rather than from activation of nociceptors. It is often associated with feelings of burning or pins and needles. These sensations can shoot down the tracts of long axons, causing great discomfort. Syndromes of neuropathic pain include reflex sympathetic dystrophy, complex regional pain syndrome, post-herpetic neuralgia after an episode of shingles, and phantom limb pain.

Can a picture of the neural activity in pain states be formed? Can we see another person's pain?

In 2013, Wager and his colleagues used fMRI to identify a 'neurologic signature' that was associated with heat-induced pain. The widespread pattern of activity included 'the thalamus, the posterior and anterior insulae, the secondary somatosensory cortex, the anterior cingulate cortex, the periaqueductal grey region,' amongst others. Social pain was found 'to activate many of the same brain regions as physical pain'.

How do we treat pain?

Since the discovery and use of the opium poppy by the Sumerians around 3300 BC, opiates have been a mainstay of pain treatment. They act by stimulating the four main classes of opiate receptors. These are widely distributed and are why the side effects of opiates are so varied. They can range from constipation to euphoria to respiratory depression.

Aspirin has also been around a while. There are Egyptian hieroglyphs detailing the use of willow bark poultices that contain aspirin, long before it was finally produced in its purified form in 1898. Drugs such as aspirin and paracetamol and other non-steroidal anti-inflammatories block the activity of the COX enzymes that produce prostaglandins from arachidonic acid and reduce the sensitisation of peripheral nociceptor activity caused by prostaglandin release.

Because chronic pain is often associated with changes in sleep pattern and mood, the tricyclic antidepressants can be very useful as an additional therapy. Because of the influence of brain stem nuclei on the dorsal horn, the selective serotonin reuptake inhibitors (SSRIs) that increase synaptic serotonin can also be used in chronic pain states. There are now useful medications that have mixed adrenergic and serotonin reuptake inhibition. The 5HT precursors, such as tryptophan, are also used in chronic pain states and migraine.

Other ways that can reduce pain include aerobic exercise, leading to increased endogenous opiate activation in the periaqueductal grey region. This kind of activity can be just as useful as antidepressants at improving mood and sleep patterns in people with chronic pain.

There are many other therapies, such as acupuncture, massage, autoregulation, meditation and mindfulness that can be beneficial. Working out which therapy is likely to be helpful to an individual is difficult.

Researching treatment effects produces lots of detail about numbers of people in the study group who have this or that effect related to this or that treatment. From this, we can work out what the probability of treatment effects is for someone having treatment. We say they have an X per cent chance of developing this or a Y per cent chance of developing that. But unfortunately, when the patient is in front of us, we cannot tell with a hundred per cent accuracy what is going to happen to them as individuals. We can only tell them the percentage risk or likelihood of something happening. There is no crystal ball. The only way to see if the treatment works is to try it. If it has worked before, it is likely to work again.

Placebo and nocebo effects

When we enter into any treatment process, we come with our own beliefs about how the world works and our place in it, our own internal narrative. These beliefs will influence the effectiveness of the treatment by a process called the ***placebo effect***. What you think will work, will. The term placebo effect also has an interesting back-story that illustrates the many historical connections between religion and medicine.

Placebo comes from the Latin verb *placere*, to please. An early use is in the cycle of prayers called The Office of the Dead. This is recited for the repose of the souls of the dead in the Roman Catholic Church. The first words of these prayers are '*Placebo domino*', meaning 'I shall please the Lord'.

By Middle English the word meant sycophant or flatterer, but by the 1700s the use of the term placebo had changed. It was now being used by physicians for drugs with no known clinical effect but that pleased the patient when they were prescribed. What could be called the 'placebo patiens' was born.

Placebo effects are mediated by neurotransmitters, such as endorphins, cannabinoids and dopamine, with activation of prefrontal cortex, anterior insula, rostral anterior cingulate cortex and amygdala (Kaptchuk and Miller, 2015).

But placebo effects are not just related to the physical effects of the chemicals. Context is important. What has been called 'the therapeutic encounter' is where and how the placebo is delivered. This is full of ritual, symbols and interactions laden with emotion which have psychosocial effects.

The role of the clinic is important. There is the ritual of making an appointment, turning up, meeting clinicians, the taking of a history and the examination. The patients bring their own beliefs and expectations into a clinical environment and are surrounded by equipment with potent symbolic meaning and power, such as stethoscopes and blood pressure machines and needles and drips. Here they engage with clinicians and other staff over matters, often, of life or death. During the processes of diagnosis and treatment, they are subject to intimate examinations, and subject to the empathy, or not, of staff. All this adds to the emotions around these events (Kaptchuk and Miller, 2015).

Placebos do have therapeutic effects. They cannot change the course of a disease. If they did, they would not be a placebo but a drug. But they can help relieve the symptoms of disease and the side effects of treatment, such as nausea, tiredness and pain. This can make the patients feel comfortable so they can have a pleasant experience.

Within medicine though, placebo effects are often considered unworthy and illegitimate. They are thought to be unscientific and caused by bias, expectation and beliefs, including prejudice. But one of the goals of medicine is to heal, and the process of healing can include cure, control of disease, and symptom relief or provision of comfort. When cure becomes impossible and control of the disease is lost, the task of medicine then becomes the relief of unnecessary suffering.

Supportive and attentive health care can create a 'therapeutic bias' in patients towards hope and a sense of relief and reprieve. Empathy from health-care staff influences those conscious and subconscious mechanisms that can drive patients to reduce the severity of their symptoms. To use the terms of cognitive psychology, healing interactions can 'frame', 'anchor' or 'nudge' patients, changing 'their perceptions of their symptoms and illness, making them less disturbed or perturbed' (Kaptchuk and Miller, 2015).

One of the 'moral imperatives' of medicine is to relieve unnecessary suffering using ways that are transparent and trustworthy. Placebo effects are not false effects — they are at the heart of medicine as a healing profession. In the future, placebo studies with correct controls for effects like spontaneous remission and regression to the mean, could measure all the various 'clinical, psychological, and biologic effects' that happen when patients are immersed in a clinical environment. A relevant question, for instance, could be: what is the most effective combination of 'attention, gaze, touch, trust, openness, confidence, thoughtful words and manner of speaking' that reduce the discomforts, the disability and the disfigurement of both disease and treatment? (Kaptchuk and Miller, 2015).

As well as providing symptom relief, placebo effects can also increase the effectiveness of drugs known to work. Rizatriptan is an effective pain-relieving drug used in the treatment of intermittent migraine. In one study, patients either took 10 mg of rizatriptan that was labelled 'placebo' or a placebo labelled 'rizatriptan' as treatment for their migraine. The outcomes were the same for both sets of patients. The rizatriptan labelled as placebo had a pure drug effect that was the same as the pure expectation effect of the placebo labelled rizatriptan. However, when the rizatriptan was correctly labelled, its clinical effect increased by fifty per cent (Kaptchuk and Miller, 2015).

Unfortunately, the same psychosocial factors that give rise to the positive effects of placebo can also give rise to negative ***nocebo effects***. The nocebo effect is the flip side of the coin to placebo. Nocebo comes from the Latin verb *nocere*, meaning to harm. It happens when a chemical with no known drug effect produces symptoms disturbing to the patient. It has been estimated in some reviews that between four and twenty-six per cent of patients randomly selected for placebo in trials discontinue it because of negative side effects.

This may happen for many reasons. Again, context is important. In a therapeutic encounter, the patient is often in an unfamiliar environment and under emotional or physical stress with time to burn. They have more time to pay attention to the usual discomforts of everyday life that would seem normal in other circumstances. This constant stress can lead to changes of mood where patients are biased to expect negative effects. This expectation bias increases the chances of them happening, as it does in the placebo effect. It may be that many of the negative side effects of medications are actually expected nocebo effects.

We have seen that these 'expectation effects' are important in other areas of perception as well. There is a need within health care to find a balance between disclosing all potential adverse effects of medications and preventing nocebo effects (Kaptchuk and Miller, 2015).

Framing — presentation influences interpretation

And finally, here is a section on how easy it is to change our perceptions or opinions by changing how information is presented, by 'framing'. In this age of 'fake news' and social media caverns and deliberate targeting of voters, it is a stark reminder of just how easy it is. And it always has been. It is frightening stuff.

The way information is presented to us is called ***framing***, and it is a major influence on the way we perceive and hence interpret information. Framing effects are where differences in presentation of the same information changes the way we interpret that information and make choices. Politicians and advertisers understand this implicitly. If you were told a drug has a 25–50% chance of causing a problem, would you take it? If you were told 50–75% of people who took the drug didn't develop a problem, would you take it then? Same drug, remember.

Framing effects were hard to remove from the early studies of risky choice. In these studies, how choices were made depended on how those choices were framed. This is illustrated in the following study, where 152 subjects were studied in the first problem, 155 in the second:

Problem 1

Imagine that the US is preparing for the outbreak of an unusual Asian disease, expected to kill 600 people. Two alternative programmes to combat the disease have been proposed. Assume that the exact scientific estimates of the consequences of the programmes are as follows:

- If programme A is adopted, 200 out of the 600 will be saved
- If programme B is adopted, there is a one-third probability that 600 people will be saved and a two-thirds probability that no one will be saved.

Which of the two programmes would you favour?

72% chose programme A; 28% chose programme B.

So, in this problem where two choices were possible, the majority preferred the certain choice where 200 lives were definitely saved, over the risky choice where there was a two-thirds probability that no lives would be saved.

Now see what happens when the problem is framed differently:

Problem 2

- If programme C is adopted, 400 people will die
- If programme D is adopted, there is a one-third probability that nobody will die, and a two-thirds probability that 600 people will die.

22% chose programme C; 78% chose programme D. So, even though programmes A and B are the same as programmes C and D, respectively, the respondents chose differently.

This is an example of a framing effect where a change from 'lives saved' to 'lives lost' produced 'a marked shift of preference from risk aversion to risk seeking'. This could mean that in this study, the subjects accepted the descriptions of the outcomes as a given, without the need for further evaluation and that they judged the outcomes simply as gains or losses only (Kahneman and Tversky, 1984).

Another framing effect is seen where information that is presented using frequency instead of probability is judged differently. Participants have been given the option to win one dollar by picking a red bean out of a bowl containing seven red beans out of a hundred beans total, or picking a red bean out of a bowl containing one in ten red beans. A majority will choose the bowl containing seven out of a 100, even though the probability of choosing a red bean from that bowl is less.

As we have seen, recall of events is better when they are framed in a story rather than presented using bar graphs (Gigerenzer, 1996). And credibility matters — who is giving us information influences whether we believe it. Consider the fact that a glass of red wine a day may be good for your health. As Jonathan Freedland wrote in the *Guardian* in 2017: Would we trust this advice if we were told by an alcoholic? Would we trust this advice if we were told by a doctor? You choose.

For us as humans, perception is all there is. It is our reality. If we *think* it is, chances are it *actually* is, but we have no way of knowing for certain. This, and the notion that time for us is limited, are two of the fundamental truths about our universe.

So, to **summarise** then: How does the process of perception work, and how does it guide behaviour? Modified signals from receptors, such as those in the retina of the eye or the basilar membrane of the ear, are eventually processed in a series of regions in the cerebral cortex to 'compute descriptions of the world: what or where objects are'. Signals are then sent from these cortical areas to other brain structures, such as the anterior cingulate cortex, that evaluate choices and compare rewards, attaching meaning to the sensory descriptions. As suggested by Conway and Rehding, decisions are eventually made 'guided by learning, memory and emotions'.

And how much is our internal narrative, that voice within,

guiding us? How much does this inner voice that is prescient all our waking day guide attention, use emotion, access memory and drive perception to achieve our goals? Fascinating stuff.

7

Summary

Here is a simple story, composed to illustrate how the components of FACE MaP could interact to produce thought and behaviour. I will call our character John.

> I stepped onto the busy escalator in the local mall, thinking about work. As I was mulling over the events of the day, about halfway up something flickered across my peripheral vision, catching my attention. My heart raced. I tensed, braced to move, and turned to look at what had caught my eye. Huh ... Yuhuk! A large, dark, stained frock coat with a bright red buttonhole was moving slowly down the other escalator, worn by someone equally large and stained by middle age, whose lower legs I could see were ravaged by ulcers.
>
> Whew! No threat there then. I relaxed and continued ruminating.
>
> At the top of the escalator I couldn't help but look at the

> corner sweet shop, laden with delicious combinations of chocolate, gelatine, sugar, flour and spices. I looked at my watch, saw I had time to spare and went in.
>
> An unexpected, pungent aroma hit me first, mainly the aniseed. Struck dumb, catching my breath, I froze. After what seemed like a lifetime, but must only have been a few seconds, I sneaked a breath, found the smell less intense, and breathed again. After a couple of minutes browsing near the door, I chose what I wanted and turned to pay.
>
> The shop counter ran along the back wall of the shop, which I hadn't noticed before, and was surrounded by shelves piled with sweets, cookies and candy bars of well-known brands. I stared, suddenly annoyed. It was the same old bloody story. Those products were backed by widespread TV advertising and given a prominent position in the shop, guaranteeing they would be sold. First of all, we are subconsciously primed by television and then gently nudged as we stare blindly at the shelves while queuing to pay.
>
> Tense and in a hurry, annoyed at being sidetracked into the shop, choosing without having a good look around, and then, worst of all, being corralled and manipulated as well, I decided I didn't want anything after all. Angry, I turned around, dumped what I had selected and stormed out, slamming the door as I went.

Can we understand what was going through John's mind?

Here is an interpretation based on the FACE MaP concept.

While conscious and awake, and riding an escalator at the local mall, John is mulling over his work. What that work is, is not disclosed. Little is known about context — such as the time restraints and goal state, as well as his mood and emotional state.

But suddenly something catches his eye. Subconscious reflex action forces John to turn and look at the same time as the automatic 'fright-and-flight' reaction starts to kick in. Suddenly he is focused and attentive and ready to flee, and there is a fast conscious analysis of the person in the frock coat. Attention, perception, emotion and episodic memory are rapidly used to determine whether there is any danger or not by judging the person to be 'good' or 'bad'. This takes one-tenth of a second.

Having rapidly perceived there was no threat, attention now shifts back to the slower, more analytical process of thinking about work. The pulse begins to slow, the muscles of flight will relax.

Now deep in thought, John continues to ride the escalator. This uses procedural memory requiring little attention and allows him to keep paying attention to what he is thinking about, as well as to carry on the journey safely. This is multitasking at its best. Looking back later, John will likely remember what was being thought about but will recall little about the actual escalator ride.

At the top of the escalator, he is again distracted, this time by a sweet shop laden with its enticing wares. Does this tell us something about his emotional state? And what is it about his attention span? Is it his personality or is it related to a heightened awareness from an anxiety state fuelled by lack of time? Or lack of food? Or wanting a token reward in a reward-free environment?

John seems to have had previous experience with sweets because they are described as being delicious. So, because there is time to spare, and perhaps because of previous conditioning by positively reinforced associative learning, or previous priming, or just simply responding to need or curiosity, he is drawn towards the shop. At another level in the hierarchy of thinking, a sub-goal has been formed. The shop must be checked out.

Now look what happens on entering the shop.

Caught unawares, the smell of aniseed is so overpowering that he suddenly freezes and stops breathing — this happens when we are exposed to a strong stimulus. We stop and don't move or breathe. This reduces our exposure and gives us time to think. Our attention is heightened automatically, and we quickly test this strong smell to see if it is noxious, using perception, memory and emotion. Then, if the stimulus is not harmful and if nothing else happens, we relax. We will become habituated, the intensity of the smell will reduce, and our attention can shift elsewhere.

John then continues with the sub-goal — to look inside the shop and maybe buy something that appeals. The decision to buy would be made from a mishmash of things like experience, maybe from previous exposure to sweets, maybe from being primed on prime-time TV, and also having the time and money available.

So, after a couple of minutes looking around, a choice is made and he turns to pay.

The counter sits amongst a confused array of shelves piled high with merchandise that he hadn't noticed previously. How did that happen? How was such an obvious feature missed? Was it because he was in such a rush? Was it inattentional blindness? Then, having just made a choice that feels good, he is suddenly confronted by more choice in an area of the shop that should have been noticed before.

A state of cognitive dissonance rapidly develops.

Because John was previously primed to want the products advertised instead of what he has chosen, his mood quickly changes. Possibly annoyed at not noticing the counter before, primed to get what is near the counter instead of what he has already got, then feeling bad about being nudged, manipulated and then trapped, and with limited time available, a good mood rapidly turns bad — and just when a good choice seemed to have been made too! The sense of loss magnifies the negative emotion felt.

At that moment, with limited time and wanting to resolve this dis-ease, John chooses the easiest way out. *The product that has been chosen is dumped and he storms out of the shop.* It would be interesting to know his thoughts and feelings at this point.

So what does this say about John's personality, his world view, his opinion of self and his internal narrative? Maybe he is having thoughts like: 'I should've known better' or 'Why didn't I just go straight to the counter?' Who knows?

All this could be interpreted from a short tale; such is the power of story. And as with most stories, it is fun speculating. With no interview or fMRI available, this is all we can do. And we do this all the time in the real world — with little available information, we try to predict interest rates, share prices, what the neighbours are arguing about and what time our partner will get home.

Was anything learned here? Would we interpret this same story differently if it was written or told to us by someone or something else in a different format in a different place? We probably would. This is due to framing. Some of the various facilities our brain has, such as consciousness and attention and internal narrative, emotion, memory and perception have been mentioned.

The first part of the book has been an attempt to understand these facilities and the processes underlying them, and how they all interact to make us do what we do, to make us human. The next part is about the structures that make this happen.

PART II

Biology of the Brain

8

Biology of the Brain

Basic nerve cell function

The brain has two main functions:

1. To maintain a healthy internal environment that keeps us alive through mechanisms called homeostasis
2. To provide the structure to respond to our external environment appropriately.

This 1.5-kilogram lump of tightly packed neural wiring is responsible for the activity produced by our minds. Sitting inside the bony cavity of the skull, like a piece of meat in a covered roasting dish, bathed in its own specialised cerebrospinal fluid (CSF) and surrounded by layers of tight membrane called dura, it is made up of billions of specialised cells called neurons, with their supporting astrocytes and glia, connective tissue and blood vessels. Neurons are the basic functional units of the brain, and they connect to form circuits that are precise at any one time. But these connections are not constant and can change over time; they are plastic.

In the late nineteenth century, the physicians Camillo Golgi in Italy and Santiago Ramón y Cajal in Spain, described neurons in detail and jointly received a Nobel Prize for Physiology or Medicine in 1906 for their work. This formed the basis of the 'neuron doctrine' — the idea that individual neurons are the elementary signalling units of the nervous system. The introduction of the electron microscope in the 1950s defined the microanatomy of the neuron even further.

The numbers are staggering. There are about one hundred different types of neuron, an estimated total of a trillion (10^{12}), with a quadrillion (10^{15}) connections. In only one cubic centimetre of grey matter there are thought to be more connections than stars in the Milky Way of our galaxy. According to Brian Appleyard, these are capable of 40 trillion synaptic firings per second, and the whole brain is able to handle the order of 10,000 trillion firings per second. The storage of memory alone in the human brain is the equivalent of 10 trillion bytes (10,000 GB, or 10 TB).

Computer simulations of the cerebral cortex of the common cat need 147,456 processors and 144 TB of working-memory. Our cerebral cortex is five to ten times larger. The eyes can transfer 72 GB of information to the brain every second, while the thalamus analyses some five million input signals per second from sensation alone.

Neurons have three fundamental properties that enable precise communication, both locally and over long distances:

1. There is a polarity between the dendrites at one end that receive inputs, and the axon-synapse end. This drives the signal in one direction only.
2. The neuron is excitable, electrically and chemically, and
3. The neuron has special secretory abilities that allow it to release neurotransmitters at synapses.

Each neuron consists of four distinct regions, each with a different function:

1. *Dendrites*. These receive inputs from the axons or dendrites of other neurons and have multiple branching connections. There can be anything from 10,000 on a single spinal motor cell to about 150,000 on a single Purkinje cell in the cerebellum.
2. *Cell body*. This keeps the neuron functioning and integrates all the inputs. The cell body has a nucleus that stores the genetic material, and a cytoplasm responsible for maintaining the structure and function of the entire neuron. It integrates the inputs coming onto the dendrites into a conductible impulse. In terms of size, the average diameter of a human hair is around 100 microns (100 thousandths of a millimetre), whereas the nerve cell body is less than 50 microns in diameter.
3. *Axon*. This conducts the impulse towards the synapses at speeds of up to 100 m/s in long motor neurons. Axons can range in width from 0.2 to about 20 microns, so between five and fifty axons can fit into one hair. They can vary in length from 0.1 mm up to two metres long and can branch many times, forming up to 1,000 connections with other axons, cell bodies or dendrites.

4. *Synapse.* This is the localised area that looks like a button under the electron microscope. It is where neurons connect and is composed of the pre-synapse, the synaptic space and the post-synapse.

Neurons work by producing voltage changes across the phospholipid membrane enclosing the nerve cell. These can then travel rapidly in waves, called impulses, down the axon in one direction. These impulses are not electrons flowing down a wire that produce a current. But they can, like electrical current, respond to electromagnetic fields. If we call the voltage on the outside of the cell membrane zero, then the voltage inside the cell is around –65 millivolts. In other words, there is a potential difference of 65 millivolts across the cell membrane.

So, how is this potential difference produced?

Inside and outside the cell are various chemicals that carry an electrical charge. They are called ions and consist of the positive ions sodium (Na+) and potassium (K+), and negatively charged amino acids and cell proteins. There is also a protein structure within the cell membrane, called the sodium-potassium pump. This keeps the concentration of potassium within the cell high, and the concentration of sodium low. The potential difference comes from the selective leakage of potassium from inside the cell outwards through small holes, called ion channels. Sodium is unable to leak inwards through these channels. The relative absence of the positive potassium inside the cell creates the negative voltage.

Each neuron acts like a filter or a gate. When the positive (excitatory) and negative (inhibitory) inputs from other axons onto the dendrites or cell body combine to produce an increase of

10 mV across the cell membrane, sodium suddenly floods into the cell. This shifts the potential difference towards zero, which then generates an action potential that is transmitted down the axon to the synapses at speeds of up to 100 m/sec.

At end of the axon, fluxes of calcium (Ca++) ions allow tiny sacks called vesicles, to release the neurotransmitters within them into the synaptic space, each vesicle containing approximately 5,000 molecules of neurotransmitters. Once released, these neurotransmitters diffuse across the synaptic space and activate post-synaptic receptors. These receptors are large proteins that are part of the next neuron in the circuit. These receptors then produce inhibitory or excitatory responses that can be summed up to determine whether or not this next neuron produces an impulse.

Neurotransmitters and the response they generate in the next cell are generally consistent, one neurotransmitter always having the same effect on the post-synaptic receptor. After release into the synaptic cleft, the transmitters are then transported back into the neuron by transport mechanisms specific to the transmitter.

There are also some atypical synaptic connections, where the transmitters that are released spread to many target areas at the same time without specific synaptic structures.

There is a beautiful simplicity to neuron organisation and brain function:

1. All neurons work in the same way to produce an electrical signal that travels, like time, in one direction.
2. Different functions are produced by the different pat-

terns of connections between nerve cells.

3. These connections are not constant. Neurons and neuronal connections changed by age, drugs, disease and trauma can again be modified with time and new experience, a concept called plasticity.

Neurons can be broadly classified into three groups:

1. Sensory neurons that convey information about the environment to the brain.
2. Motor neurons that convey information away from the brain to muscle groups and glands, producing feelings and actions.
3. Interneurons that connect with other neurons. Most neurons, particularly in the brain, are interneurons.

Neurons are mainly arranged in functional groups and systems connecting via separate pathways and acting co-operatively. For instance, there are separate systems for each of the five special senses of touch, taste, smell, hearing and vision, for sense of joint position (proprioception), and for language. In some systems and parts of systems the neurons run in parallel, so these systems can be used with other systems, or parts of other systems, to perform different functions at the same time. In other systems the neurons run end on end in series, and these systems can only do one thing at time.

These systems are hierarchical — from the periphery, to the spinal cord, to the brain stem, to the nuclei in midbrain and cerebral hemispheres, to areas of the cerebral cortex — adding layers of bottom-up complexity in information processing. Higher levels of function would include thinking, deciding and consciousness. Perception has some higher-level capability, but most of the time it functions at the same level as attention, memory and emotion. These systems can be influenced by either bottom-up or top-down modulation at any stage, in many ways: by single neurons or large systems, by nuclei, or by external influences such as electromagnetic fields, the insertion of electrodes, by chemicals or by trauma.

There are many hidden relationships between the seemingly unconnected, and it is a two-way street. For instance, endorphins produced by aerobic exercise are released into the periaqueductal grey matter in the brain stem, influencing the lateral spinothalamic tract carrying sensation in the spinal cord from the periphery to the thalamus. This changes pain perception. Mood and sleep patterns are also improved. It seems counter-intuitive to think that regular aerobic exercise can make you feel less depressed, can improve your sleep patterns and improve muscular pain in areas not being exercised. There are many other modulating influences, where small numbers of neurons can have major influences on brain function.

All this uses energy, the brain consuming 20–40% of the body's energy needs at any one time, so there are default systems or shortcuts that exist to make the brain work more efficiently. For instance, when we use memory we have ways of using it quickly that may produce some errors but work well for us most of the time. These supposed errors are deviations from what is expected from normative theory, or deviations from the norm, and were initially described by cognitive scientists.

They can now be explained by neuroscience:

- Memories can be recalled subconsciously.

- Recent memories are accessed faster than older memories.
- During recall, the memories recalled *first* influence the recall of other memories.

The 'availability heuristic' described by Tversky and Kahneman in 1974, and the effect of priming on decision-making, both depend on these properties of memory.

Structure

The nervous system can be roughly divided up into the *peripheral nervous system* and the *central nervous system,* which includes the spinal cord, the brain and cranial nerves. These regions are all heavily interdependent, each affecting, or modulating, the activities of the others.

Tissue inside the brain can be roughly divided into areas of grey matter and areas of white matter:

- The main areas of grey matter are the covering cortex and nuclei, like the amygdala, thalamus and basal ganglia. Nuclei are areas of grey matter packed with nerves with many interconnections between varieties of different cells, enabling rapid and efficient information processing.
- White matter consists of nerve axons wrapped in fatty myelin to transmit nerve impulses up to the 100 m/sec required to move from areas in the cortex to distant muscles.

As it has evolved, the structure of the human brain can be likened to a small holiday house at the beach that has been slowly added onto over a period of years. The *older brain*, sometimes called the reptilian brain, includes the brain stem, cerebellum, the hypothalamus, thalamus, basal ganglia and amygdala. Closely connected in the medial hemispheres are areas like the hippocampus and the cingulate gyrus, and in the lateral aspect, the insular cortex. This compact older brain keeps us alive and can rapidly process information, giving us a quick 'yes' or 'no' answer, very useful in times of danger or uncertainty. A lot of this rapid analysis uses areas involved with emotion, such as the amygdala and hippocampus, and mediated by the brain stem nuclei.

Wrapped over this core is the multilayered *cerebral cortex*, which has grown outwards as it has evolved, like an expanding cauliflower. Like the cauliflower head is attached to its stem, so too is the cerebral cortex attached to its own brain stem. The massive newer brain or neo-cortex, more complex than anything previous, helps modern humans reason, create and speak in complex language. Part of this large forward expansion is the frontal lobe, the largest lobe in the human brain that brings its executive prowess to brain function.

As it has enlarged, the cortex has maintained its connections with the brain stem like the cauliflower; for example, the raphe nuclei and the nucleus coeruleus, which are involved in feelings, send projections to the farthest reaches of this cortex. This overall structure gives the cerebral cortex an independence and allows it to slowly grind away when analytical thought is needed, knowing all the housekeeping is being done, and at the same time allowing attention to be accessed quickly if needed.

If we look at an isolated brain on the bench or in a diagram, the main areas of the brain that can be seen from the outside are:

- The brain stem
- The cerebellum
- The cerebral hemispheres.

Within the spinal cord, sensory impulses move up the spinal cord into the ***brain stem***, and motor signals move down through the brain stem into the spinal cord in the corticospinal tracts, eventually affecting the muscles that make us move.

The brain stem is connected at its lower end to the spinal cord and consists of three separate regions:

- The medulla
- The pons
- The midbrain.

The *medulla* is essentially similar to the spinal cord, involved in sensory and motor control of the head, neck and face.

The *pons* is an expansion of the upper brain stem, and is associated with relay of information about sensation and movement between the cerebral cortex and the cerebellum.

The *midbrain* is the junction between the brain stem and the rest of the brain. It is a small region with a complex system of nuclei and multiple tracts passing through it. It consists of a small, central CSF-filled channel called the cerebral aqueduct, with the tectum posterior to this and the tegmentum anterior to it. It plays a large part in auditory processing and behavioural responses to the environment, and contains important nuclei concerned with emotion, amongst many other capabilities. There is also an area of grey tissue surrounding the cerebral aqueduct called the periaqueductal grey which plays a large part in pain modification and mood.

As well as conveying messages to and from the spinal cord, the brain stem facilitates reflex activity between the cranial nerves and the brain stem. This is similar to reflex activity that can occur between the peripheral nervous system and the spinal cord. It also controls basic body functions such as breathing, swallowing, heart rate, blood pressure and arousal. The brain stem also uses several small groups of neurons that project widely using monoamine and acetylcholine neurotransmitters to co-ordinate central nervous system activity.

Some of these are involved in influencing pain perception and regulating the autonomic nervous system to maintain the internal environment; some are important in regulating arousal. When they act together, they can influence attention, mood and memory. The brain stem is part of our primitive brain, but projections 'from this region enable and modulate many of the higher order behaviours we regard as most human' (Kandel, 2013).

The ***cerebellum*** lies on the dorsal aspect near the top end of the brain stem. This important mushroom-type structure has a pedicle, or stem, containing all the neurons going into and out of the cerebellum, and two lobes on top of the pedicle. The cerebellum is a smaller version of the larger cerebral hemispheres and is largely responsible for movement. The two lobes are covered by the *cerebellar cortex*, very similar to the folded cortex that covers the cerebral hemispheres.

On top of the brain stem lies the *hypothalamus*, part of the diencephalon of the brain that helps to control our internal environment — the continuous regulation of internal variables, like temperature, blood pressure and blood sugar — within well-defined limits through processes collectively called homeostasis. These processes are what keep us alive 24 hours a day, regulating our appetites and needs. All cells within our body need a consistent environment to work effectively, and the hypothalamus helps achieve this.

Above the hypothalamus lie the nuclei of the *thalamus*, the other part of the diencephalon. The structure of the thalamus is a good example of the complexity and interconnectivity within the nuclei of the brain. The thalamus is an almond-shaped structure approximately two centimetres wide — there are two thalami lying next to each other — surrounded by the cerebral hemispheres on top of the brain stem. Part of their function is to convey modified sensory information to the cerebral cortex.

Within each thalamus there are up to 50 different nuclei divided into four groups, each having different roles. There are inputs directly from the retina of the eye, from the hypothalamus and the midbrain, as well as the hippocampus, the amygdala, basal ganglia, cerebellum and the cortex, including the frontal cortex. There are projections to many areas of the cortex, including the sensory and motor areas, and the frontal cortex. This enables the thalamus to play a part in memory and emotion, vision and motor control, and the sensation of pain.

These connections enable the thalamus to be more than a relay station. A large amount of information processing is available through local processing within the thalamus, with modulation by inputs coming from the brain stem and inhibition and excitation by other nuclei. It acts as a gatekeeper that can prevent or enhance 'the passage of specific information depending on our behavioural state' (Kandel, 2013). Near the thalamus are several nuclei with important roles in motor learning and control of movement, the basal ganglia, and the nucleus concerned with emotion, the amygdala.

The left and right ***cerebral hemispheres*** form the largest part of the brain and are wrapped over the brain stem and thalamus, basal ganglia and amygdala, like ice cream on a cone, each hollowed out by an H-shaped fluid-filled space called the ventricle. The cerebral hemispheres are involved in attention, perception, memory and emotion, and executive processes like planning and carrying out actions.

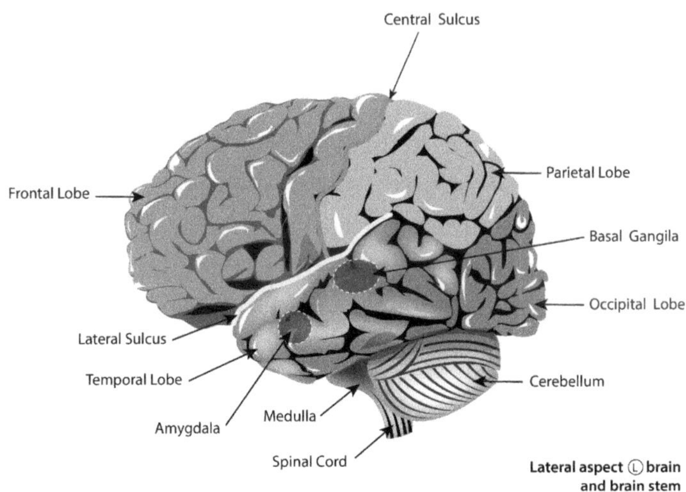

Figure 4. Lateral aspect (left) brain and brain stem

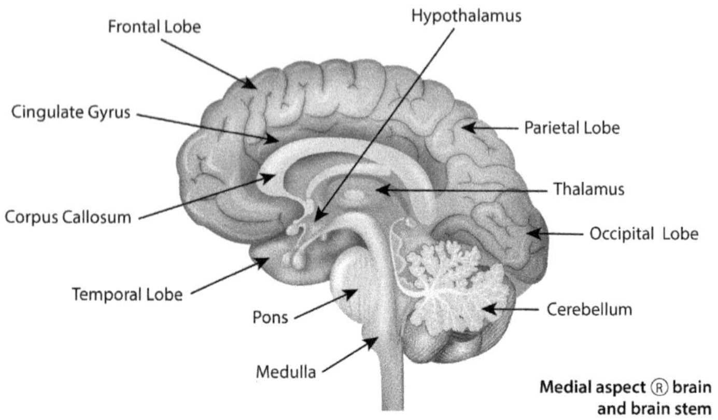

Figure 5. Medial aspect (right) brain and brain stem

The two cerebral hemispheres are connected to each other via a massive sheet of white fibres, the corpus callosum. Sensory and motor fibres cross over so that the right side of the brain controls the left side of the body. Most of us are dominant in using one hand or the other. But both hemispheres do similar things, and the ability to analyse faces, artistic ability, spatial discrimination and the processing of vision and sound are generally done bilaterally.

There is lateralisation for some functions such as language, speech and visuospatial information. This is mainly produced by left-brain activity in right-handed people, and these people tend to be more logical and systematic in their thinking. It also said that right-brain-dominant people, the left-handers, are more creative and intuitive, although these traits aren't fixed. Both right- and left-hand-dominant people can become ambidextrous.

The cerebral cortex is made of six layers, each connecting with different parts of the brain — the surface layers connect locally, and the deeper neurons connect with deeper and more distant structures. This complex carpet of grey matter covers both cerebral hemispheres and is folded to increase the amount of cortex available for analysis and computing. This ability is further increased by having six layers of varying thickness arranged in functional columns.

In general, layers of cortex cover the corresponding lobe. These areas of cortex are named from the bones of the skull that overlie them. For instance, the *frontal cortex* covers the *frontal lobe* and sits behind the *frontal bones* of the skull. The *prefrontal cortex* is the most *forward* portion of the cortex, lying just above our eyes in the front part of the frontal cortex. Both of these areas extend medially, laterally, dorsally and ventrally, to cover the whole of the front of the hemisphere:

- Ventral means facing down
- Dorsal means facing up (think dorsal fin)
- Medial means facing towards the middle
- Lateral means facing towards the outside.

On the upper part of the lateral surface of the hemispheres, behind the frontal cortex, is a deep almost vertical groove called the central sulcus. This separates the posterior frontal cortex from the parietal cortex. Deep within this sulcus is an area called the insular cortex. This is overhung by areas of cortex called the temporal operculum and the frontal operculum. The lower, diagonal, lateral sulcus is another deep groove in the lateral cortex, separating the frontal cortex from the temporal cortex. Posterior to the temporal and parietal cortical areas is the occipital cortex.

These areas of cortex wrap over the top, around the front and underneath the cerebral hemispheres to cover most of the medial aspect of the cerebral hemispheres. On this medial aspect, below the areas of cortex that wrap over the top of the hemispheres, is a curving cingulate sulcus. Below this again, the cingulate gyrus that contains the important cingulate cortex, curves over the corpus callosum. Below the corpus callosum, in the lower portion of the medial aspect of the cerebral hemispheres, in close association with the amygdala and the basal ganglia, moving from the front to the back are: the entorhinal cortex, the hippocampal formation and the parahippocampal cortex.

Different areas of the cortex are concerned with different functions; those dealing with the initial analysis of sensory data — the primary areas — and those dealing with figuring out what it all means — the association areas. The primary somatosensory cortex, dealing with sensations from the soma, or organs including the skin, lies in the anterior edge of the parietal cortex. In front of it lies the primary motor cortex. Association areas in the parietal cortex represent both internal and external space, and this representation can be modified by experience.

Also:

- Areas for speech and language lie in the temporal and frontal cortex of the left hemisphere.
- The primary visual cortex is in the occipital lobe.
- The visual association areas lie next door in the posterior parietal lobes.
- The large frontal lobe with its covering cortex is the biggest lobe by volume.

Function

So how does the brain do things? Physical properties of matter, such as vibration and temperature, are converted by our peripheral sensory receptors into neural signals that travel into the spinal cord and then centrally, via five tracts, terminating in different areas of the brain. Impulses within these long myelinated neurons travel at speeds of up to 100 m/s.

Sensory information from vision comes directly into the thalamus, and sensory information from taste and hearing comes into the brain stem directly via the cranial nerves that enter through holes in the skull. The thalamus allows some signals to be passed on and some to be blocked, depending on our mood at the time. These signals can be then passed through other nuclei or direct to areas of the cortex where they can be processed further. Some of this processing produces movement without immediate awareness, but most of it involves the conscious production of a percept, our own interpretation of what has stimulated us.

The frontal cortex, influenced by current mood, emotional state, consciousness and our internal narrative, using attention with the help of memory, is involved in producing this percept. Once it is formed, plans are made, compatible with the goal state and our inner voice, and appropriate signals are sent to execute those plans. This can take milliseconds. If a threshold for action is exceeded, signals are transmitted down long myelinated motor neurons into the spinal cord and to the appropriate muscles, to produce the appropriate action. The largest of these motor tracts, the white corticospinal tract, can be seen with the naked eye in a sectioned brain.

9

Glossary of Important Structures and Their Functions

The following glossary has largely been based on *Principles of Neural Science, Fifth Edition* (2013), edited by Eric Kandel, James Schwartz, Thomas Jessell, Steven Siegelbaum and A J Hudspeth.

Amygdala: Buried within the temporal lobe, and close to other major areas on the medial aspect of the cerebral hemispheres, such as the hippocampus, this nucleus has a major role in the emotional interpretation of what's going on around us. It is discussed in more detail in the section on emotion.

As part of the circuitry involved in the processing of conditioned and unconditioned fear, it has connections with the hypothalamus and periaqueductal grey region in the brain stem.

It also has important connections to the ventral region of the anterior cingulate cortex, the insular cortex and the VMPFC, as part of more complex emotional states, such as empathy and guilt, in contrast to its involvement in primary emotions, such as fear, pleasure or sadness. These complex emotional states produce important contributions to normal social interactions and are 'responsible for bodily changes and behaviours that are experienced consciously as distinct feelings' (Kandel, 2013).

Anterior Cingulate Gyrus (ACG) and the Anterior Cingulate Cortex (ACC): This runs above the corpus callosum on the medial aspect of each hemisphere. It has two functional subdivisions. The rostral and ventral subdivision is thought to be involved with emotional processing and mood, and autonomic function with extensive connections to the hippocampus, amygdala, VMPFC, anterior insula and nucleus accumbens. The caudal subdivision of the ACG is thought to be associated with cognitive processes involving control of behaviour, and is connected to DLPFC, the secondary motor cortex and the posterior cingulate cortex.

The ACG may help to analyse whether behaviour is progressing towards the successful completion of goals but also, when there are perceived differences between behaviour and goal state, may lead to depression. In some patients with depression, decreasing activity in some areas of the ACG is strongly associated with treatment success.

Autonomic Motor System: This system regulates homeostasis, the involuntary functions of the body that keep us alive — heart rate, breathing, digestion, sweating etc. The system consists of the hypothalamus as the main regulator, the sympathetic nervous system and the parasympathetic nervous system.

Basal Ganglia: These consist of the caudate nucleus and putamen (collectively called the striatum), the globus pallidus, subthalamic nucleus and substantia nigra, and are buried deep in the cerebral hemispheres close to the thalamus. This is a group of important, heavily interconnected nuclei with a major role in many aspects of movement, as well as regulation of eye movements, mood, reward and executive function.

Basal Nucleus of Meynert: This a group of modulatory cholinergic neurons located beneath the basal ganglia with projections to most areas of the neocortex, and is involved in arousal and attention, along with the RN and LC described below.

Broca's Area: This area of lateral frontal cortex in the left hemisphere controls the production of intelligent speech. It is situated near the area of the motor cortex that controls the mouth and tongue movements forming words. It is heavily linked to Wernicke's area in the left inferior parietal lobe by a bidirectional pathway.

Cerebral Cortex: Information from all sources will at some stage arrive at the cerebral cortex. This rumpled layer of grey matter covers both cerebral hemispheres and is mainly concerned with cognition — the production of thoughts. It is different to the cerebellar cortex which is largely involved in movement. The word cerebral itself means 'that involving intelligence or intellect' rather than that involving emotion or instinct.

Overall, the cerebral cortex is between two and four millimetres thick, this thickness being constant amongst various regions of each brain and also amongst the brains of other species. If you look at the outside of the brain, the cerebral cortex is crumpled up into grooves, or sulci, and rounded prominent gyri. Like the layers of silicon on the embryo computer chip, this crumpling increases the surface area and volume of the cortex, giving the brain more power. It is an organic computer.

The basic structure of the cortex consists of six layers, each layer having specific connections and defined histologically by the presence or absence of neuronal cell bodies.

Layer I: Outer molecular layer
Layer II: External granular cell layer
Layer III: External pyramidal cell layer
Layer IV: Internal granular cell layer
Layer V: Internal pyramidal cell layer
Layer VI: Polymorphic or multiform layer

'Ascending or feed-forward pathways generally originate in the more superficial Layers I to III and invariably terminate in Layer IV, whereas descending or feed-back pathways generally originate in the deeper Layers V and VI and terminate in Layers I and IV' (Kandel, 2013).

Different parts of the cerebral cortex have layers of different thickness. As sensory information from the thalamus generally enters at Layer IV, areas of sensory cortex concerned largely with *inputs,* such as the primary visual cortex at the back of the brain, have a much thicker Layer IV. Areas concerned mainly with *outputs,* such as the primary motor cortex, have a thinner Layer IV and a much thicker Layer V, one of the prominent output layers.

There are two main types of neuron in the cerebral cortex:

1. The projection neurons have pyramidal-shaped cell

bodies, located mainly in the pyramidal Layers III and V, and also VI. The primary neurotransmitter used by this neuron is the excitatory amino acid, glutamine.

2. The interneurons have cell bodies located in all layers, and the predominant neurotransmitter is the inhibitory gamma amino butyric acid (GABA). Several types of these interneurons have been identified according to the pattern of their connections to other cell bodies, or axons, such as basket cells and chandelier cells, and their co-transmitters, neuroactive peptides such as endorphins.

So why have a layered cortex?

The layering of neurons appears to be an efficient way of organising the input-output relationships in ways that are only now becoming more fully understood. *Inputs* to the cortex come from the thalamus, other cortical areas on both sides of the brain and other areas such as the basal ganglia and brain stem. *Outputs* from the cortex go to other areas of the cortex on both sides of the brain, the basal ganglia, thalamus, pontine nuclei in the brain stem and to the spinal cord. Different inputs are processed in different ways, and outputs come from different populations of neurons.

The neurons in the cortex are arranged in columns, each neuron within the column having similar properties and each column forming a local processing network, the fundamental computational units of the cortex. A column has a diameter of around 100 microns. All columns form parts of larger functional groups. In 1909, Korbinian Brodmann divided the cerebral cortex into 47 different regions based on microscopic characteristics of the different areas. This is still in use today but has been further subdivided as we have come to know more. Some of these regions are primary functional areas where information is first received, processed and then sent on to other association areas for further processing. Association areas are regions where information that has already been processed is refined again.

There are four main areas of neocortex in the human, referenced to the bones overlying them:

1. Frontal
2. Temporal
3. Occipital
4. Parietal

One of the important landmarks is the central fissure or sulcus. Along with the lateral sulcus, it separates the frontal lobe from the other three areas of cortex behind it. These three could be called the TOP areas, and their functions are different from those of the frontal lobe. The TOP neurons are devoted primarily to perception and long-term memory.

The primary sensory cortices of all sense modalities are located in the TOP as well as their areas of association cortex. Sensory information is initially decoded in the primary cortex then assembled and assimilated in the association areas. The TOP is also the site of long-term memory storage. The frontal cortex is deeply involved in emotional responses, working-memory, attention, personality and memory recall. These are useful abilities for any executive (Dietrich, 2004).

So we have two important brain regions that can change the way we perceive information: the gatekeeper — the thalamus — and the computer — the cortex. These also form part of the systems related to attention, emotion and memory, which all interact to produce a percept that helps us explain the world based on our own experience.

Entorhinal Cortex: This is part of the medial temporal lobe lying within the parahippocampal gyrus, close to the hippocampus. It acts as a major gateway to the hypothalamus for highly processed sensory information and ongoing cognitive processes. It contains grid cells that, along with place cells in the hippocampus, play an important role in the production of spatial memory.

Fusiform Gyrus: This is in the inferior temporal lobe and it plays a role in recognition of face.

Hippocampus: This is an area of the inferior medial cerebral hemisphere and it plays a large role in the co-ordination of memory processes.

First described in the sixteenth century, the hippocampus is a ridge running along the floor of the temporal horn of the lateral ventricle in the lower part of the temporal lobe, near the amygdala. It is covered by the parahippocampal gyrus on the outside. When removed from the brain, it looks like a seahorse, hence its name.

The hippocampal formation includes the hippocampal regions CA1 through to 4 and the dentate gyrus, with other regions like the entorhinal cortex and the subiculum lying nearby in the parahippocampal gyrus. The precise details of the structure and function of these areas is still being debated. The letters CA are an abbreviation of cornu Ammonis, the horn of Amun, the ancient Egyptian god who was often represented as having a ram's head. Ram's head is an older name for the hippocampus.

The entorhinal cortex is a link between the hippocampus and the rest of the brain. It receives highly processed inputs from every sensory modality, from areas of association cortex as well as inputs related to ongoing cognitive processes via the prefrontal cortex. In addition to highly processed information, it also receives inputs for brain stem nuclei, such as the locus coeruleus and raphe nuclei and nuclei within the thalamus and hypothalamus. The output to the hippocampus is via the perforant pathway.

Other inputs to the hippocampus come from the dopamine, serotonin and noradrenalin systems, together with the medial septal nucleus. These inputs modulate the activity of the hippocampus. Outputs from the hippocampus go largely to the entorhinal cortex as well as the medial prefrontal cortex and the mammillary body of the hypothalamus and lateral septal area.

The hippocampus can be divided into dorsal, intermediate and ventral areas. The dorsal hippocampus is involved in spatial and verbal memory and the learning of new concepts. It has the highest concentration of place cells. The ventral area is involved with fear conditioning, including the emotional responses of our experiences in episodic memory. The intermediate area overlaps both the dorsal and ventral areas and has links to the medial prefrontal cortex (Wikipedia, accessed 2018).

Information from the entorhinal cortex is projected through an indirect and direct pathway onto CA1 region of the hippocampus, possibly allowing comparison of information from the indirect pathway with information from sensory input via the direct pathway. The direct pathway originates in neurons of Layer III of the entorhinal cortex, projecting directly onto CA1 apical dendrites.

The indirect pathway is more complex. Neurons from Layer II of the entorhinal cortex project onto the granule cells of the dentate gyrus. The axons of these granule cells run in the mossy fibre pathway and excite pyramidal cells in the CA3 region of the hippocampus. Axons from these CA3 pyramidal cells run through the Schaffer collateral pathway and excite regions of CA1 pyramidal cell dendrites. These synapse close to the cell body when compared to axons of the direct pathway.

Lesions in *indirect* pathways can cause problems with complex spatial learning and memory tasks, while lesions in the *direct* pathway can cause problems with consolidation of long-term memory. The CA1 region of the hippocampus also projects back to layers in the entorhinal cortex and nearby subiculum.

Hypothalamus: This sits on top of the brain stem and is responsible for regulating the internal environment keeping the brain and the body alive. A major part of the autonomic nervous system that projects onto internal organs, such as the heart and the gut, producing those feelings we label as affect, our innate response to emotion.

Insular Cortex: This hidden area of cortex lies on the junction of the frontal and temporal lobes, overlying the lateral aspect of the putamen. It is a region involved with emotional processing, along with the amygdala, the VMPFC and the anterior cingulate cortex. Sectors 'that are activated during recall of emotional feelings are also activated during the conscious sensation of pain and temperature.' There are also suggestions 'that the insular cortices play a role in associating external cues with internal states such as pleasure and desire' and play a role in maintaining addictive states (Kandel, 2013).

Limbic system: This term was introduced by Pierre Paul Broca in the mid-19th century to describe portions of the frontal, temporal and parietal lobes encircling the ventricles — the fluid-filled portions of the brain. It basically consists of the hippocampal formation and cingulate gyrus. This term is not used very often now.

Locus Coeruleus (LC): Located within the large bulge in the brain stem called the pons, this is part of a group of brain stem neurons modulating attention and arousal. Neurons projecting from the LC use the monoamine neurotransmitter noradrenalin (nor-A, norepinephrine). The other major site of nor-A production is in the adrenal gland.

The LC has a number of inputs, including the medial prefrontal cortex, the hypothalamus and the cingulate gyrus, the amygdala, the cerebellum and the raphe nucleus. This allows emotion, pain and stress to produce a reaction mediated by adrenergic neurons, in some situations called the fright-and-flight reaction. Neurons projecting from the LC connect in turn to the cortex, the amygdala, the ventral tegmental area, the thalamus, hypothalamus, cerebellum and brain stem and spinal cord, amongst others. Descending projections onto the dorsal horn of the spinal cord influence pain perception.

Nucleus Accumbens (NAc): This is part of the dopaminergic circuits relating to reward, including the medial prefrontal cortex and the ventral tegmental area in the brain stem, and it lies in the basal forebrain in front of the hypothalamus. The NAc and the olfactory tubercle form the ventral striatum portion of the basal ganglia.

Raphe Nuclei (RN): These are another part of a group of upper brain stem neurons modulating attention and arousal. Located along a strip of the medial brain stem, there are up to seven named raphe nuclei that make up the medial portion of the reticular activating system and have a widespread influence on brain function.

Because of their location and length, these small areas of RN collectively receive from and project to most areas of the brain. Numerous inputs onto the dorsal raphe nucleus — for example from the frontal cortex, cingulate cortex and several areas of the hypothalamus — influence mood states, such as depression, and anxiety states, such as obsessive-compulsive disorder.

Projection neurons from the more rostral end of the brain stem mainly use the monoamine neurotransmitter, serotonin, and project to the higher centres, whilst projection neurons from the more caudal nuclei project to the lower brain stem and the dorsal horn of the spinal cord. In the spinal cord they reduce responses to noxious stimuli and so influence pain perception.

Many projection neurons from the RN also use the widespread neurotransmitter and chemical messenger dopamine.

The site and function of the raphe nuclei and the locus coeruleus show why our emotional responses are so innate and rapid, and are such an important core component of our lizard brain.

Retina: Visible light is converted into neural impulses through a process called phototransduction. The conversion begins in the retina at the back of the eye. All visual experience is based on this neural circuit in the eye that is the 'brain's window on the world. The retina's output is conveyed to the brain by just one million optic nerve fibres, and yet almost half of the cerebral cortex is used to process these signals'. Some of the initial visual information is lost by processing within the retina and 'can never be recovered' (Kandel, 2013).

The retina is a 'thin sheet of neurons, a few hundred micrometres thick, composed of five major cell types arranged in three cellular layers, separated by two synaptic layers'. This wraps around the back of the eye covering most of the globe, extending from the iris backwards. The photoreceptor cells in the outermost layer absorb light and convert it to a neural signal by phototransduction.

There are two types of receptor cells in the retina — rods and cones — and each acts as a filter for a narrow range of bandwidth of light. Receptors are tuned to an optimal frequency that 'activates the receptor at low energy and evokes the strongest response'.

Rods work well in dim light and occur mainly on the periphery of the retina, increasing our peripheral vision in the dark. A few millimetres outside the central fovea rods outnumber cones, and all photoreceptors become larger and more widely spaced towards the periphery. Impulses from many rods connect to a single ganglion that fire only when enough impulses have arrived, acting as an efficient filter. Rods are extremely sensitive to light and can pick up a single photon, but as the level of light increases the rods respond less to variations in intensity.

There are three types of *cones*, each with a particular sensitivity to a certain band of visible light between the wavelengths of around 400 to 700 nm: the S, short wavelength, or blue, cones that are most sensitive to light around 437 nm; the M, medium wavelength, or green, cones that are most sensitive to light around 533 nm; and L, long wavelength, or red, cones that are most sensitive to light around 564 nm. But there is a graded photosensitivity of these photoreceptors, enabling us to perceive a wide range of colours through varying combinations of photoreceptors.

For instance, at a wavelength of 520 nm, which is the preferred wavelength of the green cones, the blue cones don't respond at all and the red cones only respond very weakly, enabling the eye to 'see' the colour green. At a wavelength of 600 nm in the orange part of the spectrum, blue cones are not activated, the green cones respond weakly and the red cones are activated strongly, enabling us to 'see' the combination of red and green that is orange.

These cones are concentrated in the fovea in the centre of the back of the retina and generally only one cone connects with one ganglion cell. This enables our central vision to be crisper and clearer and less ambiguous, and loaded towards seeing in daylight. At night time the central fovea is blind due to the absence of rods. To see something at night we must look to one side of the object, a fact that astronomers know well when looking at the stars. If an object is focused on in poor light it disappears, and then returns when we look away.

As well as the vertical pathway between the outer layers of the retina and the ganglion cells, there are 'many lateral connections provided by the horizontal cells in the outer synaptic layer and the amacrine cells in the inner synaptic layer'. This enables the retinal circuit to perform low level visual processing, extracting 'from the raw images in the left and right eyes certain spatial and temporal features'.

This is the initial stage in the analysis of visual images, the rules of which change as the retina adjusts its sensitivity to the 'ever changing conditions of illumination' (Kandel, 2013).

See also information on Light in the Definitions section next.

Thalamus: For neuroscientists, two important areas of the brain involved with perception are the thalamus and the cerebral cortex. The thalamus acts like a sorting house, a gatekeeper, filtering out information and relaying it to the appropriate parts of the cortex for further analysis. Some information is lost. The thalamus is an almond-shaped structure approximately one to two centimetres in width. There are two lying next to each other, surrounded by the cerebral hemispheres on top of the brain stem above the hypothalamus. Part of their function is to convey modified sensory information to the cerebral cortex.

Within each thalamus there are up to 50 different nuclei divided into four groups, each having different roles. The anterior group receives information from the hypothalamus and the hippocampus and may play a part in memory and emotion. The medial group receives inputs from the amygdala, basal ganglia and midbrain and subdivisions that project to different areas of the frontal cortex. It may play a role in memory. The nuclei of the ventral group convey information from the basal ganglia and cerebellum to the motor cortex, as well as sensory information to the sensory areas of the cortex.

Visual information is received by the lateral geniculate nucleus of the thalamus and transmitted to the visual cortex. There is also a thin outer reticular layer covering the whole thalamus that consists purely of connections between different regions. This shows that the thalamus is not just a relay station. A large amount of information processing is available within the thalamus. It acts as a gatekeeper that can prevent or enhance 'the passage of specific information depending on our behavioural state' (Kandel, 2013).

Ventral Tegmental Area: This is a diffuse area lying on top of the brain stem in the midbrain, above the pons and behind the hypothalamus. It is a source of dopaminergic neurons in the brain and is implicated in the natural reward circuitry of the brain. It plays a role in motivation and orgasm.

Ventral Striatum: This consists of the nucleus accumbens and olfactory tubercle.

Wernicke's Area: An area in the inferior aspect of the left parietal lobe close to the auditory cortex, that helps process the auditory input for language. It an important area for understanding speech and is linked to Broca's area by a bidirectional pathway.

10

Definitions

Here are some definitions to clarify certain words. Many of these terms, such as intuitive thinking, are used in different ways by different authors. The definitions following are those I have used in this book.

Action: This word is used to describe any physical activity that can be measured. It is similar to behaviour. Some actions, such as reflex action, can be produced without any brain involvement, but most action is related to activity in the brain.

Affect: Affect is how we feel about something. Is it good or bad? It is our body's response to emotion generated within the brain as a reaction to a particular situation.

Attention: Attention is the 'bright light' of focused consciousness. We have to be awake to be attentive, and attention can flutter around, changing quickly, but can only focus on one thing at a time.

Behaviour: Co-ordinated action of a group of muscles that can be defined, such as sticking your tongue out at a naughty grandchild, driving a car, making a choice.

Bias: Bias is defined in the *Collins English Dictionary* as: 'an extraneous latent influence on, unrecognised conflated variable in, or selectivity in, a sample which influences its distribution and so renders it unable to reflect the desired population parameters'. Bias distorts and corrupts information and can lead to incorrect thoughts, decisions and actions. Bias in psychology usually means that which is departing from the expected norm.

Caudal: Literally means 'pointing towards the tail'. Because the axis of the brain tilts 90 degrees above the brain stem, areas that are caudal aren't always 'below' (cf. rostral).

Claustrum: A heavily connected small nucleus underlying the cerebral cortex near the insula, lying close to the white fibres under the cortex. It has been called the neuronal Grand Central and may play a cornerstone role in the production of consciousness.

Cognition: Any higher level neural processes involved in thinking.

Communication: The process of transmitting chunks of information to another person using neural activity. For us to communicate, the neural activity in our own brain has to produce various behaviours that trigger neural activity in someone else's brain.

Conscious: The state of wakefulness, awareness or arousal. Thinking as described in this book is neural activity when we are in a conscious state. Neural activity classed as subconscious or implicit is where we are conscious but not attentive.

Consciousness: All our states of feeling or sentience or awareness. Beware, this word means many things to many different people. For an interesting discussion on 'consciousness', read John Searle's 'Theory of Mind and Darwin's Legacy' in the 18 June 2013 supplement at http://www.pnas.org/content/110/Supplement_2/10343.

CT (Computed Tomography) Scan: In CT scanning of the human body, X-ray beams are fired at the area being looked at generating images depending on the ability of the tissues in the area under investigation to block the X-ray beam. Many X-ray images taken around a single axis of rotation produce cross-sectional images that are slices, or tomograms, of the areas under study. Further digital processing generates a three-dimensional image from the large series of two-dimensional images. The main problem with CT scanning is that it exposes the subject to a large amount of radiation.

Cue: A cue is generally regarded as a complex package of stimuli. The word cue can include all those stimuli except simple sensory stimuli. A 'cue' includes stimuli that are 'perceptual', 'semantic' or 'conceptual'. They can be either weak or strong, depending on their relationship with what's being perceived.

Perceptual cues — External sensory information can be interpreted via the thalamus, linking to areas involved in memory and emotion, and converted into 'perceptual cues'. Information from our eyes is quickly interpreted to produce vision.

Semantic cues can be external or produced internally and are those related to memory for events, names or words. Thinking of an event or a word or a person can influence the way we think. Some contexts will prime us to think of a particular word.

Conceptual cues can also be external or internal. They are more abstract, often involving thinking and working-memory. The memory that is used can be implicit or explicit. We develop concepts to interpret the world in our own way, and then use these concepts to modify our actions in a particular situation or explain our actions at a later time.

Domain (of Knowledge): A portion of our total knowledge that we use within a particular context, e.g. the domain of medicine, the domain of loss, or the domain of gains.

EEG (Electroencephalogram): EEGs are the extracellular recordings of the field potentials from large numbers of neurons, produced by electrodes placed on the surface of the scalp, instead of directly onto brain tissue. Field potentials are recorded as spikes in activity against the background recording. Because the recordings are from the surface of the scalp, neurons closest to the electrodes will contribute the most to the recording. So the majority of the activity measured in an EEG is from the cortex, not from underlying structures such as the brain stem, thalamus, etc. The EEG shows patterns of activity that can be associated with different states of sleep and wakefulness, such as REM sleep or stage four sleep, and some pathological states such as epilepsy.

Electrophysiological Techniques: Techniques for investigating individual neuron function use small hollow glass tubes around one micron in diameter, called pipettes that are filled with an electrolyte solution. These can be placed inside or outside the neuron and function as electrodes. They are connected to a measuring device that records the changes in voltage caused by the movement of ions across the cell membrane. They can measure single cell changes or multiple cell changes depending on their positioning. Larger electrodes are used to measure local field potentials, which are produced by the activity of larger numbers of neurons. Still larger electrodes, such as uninsulated needles and surface electrodes, are used by clinical and surgical neurophysiologists. These are only sensitive to certain types of synchronous activity within groups of millions of cells.

Emotion: Activity of the amygdala triggered by context, information or need, producing a 'good' or 'bad' response and leading to the formation of feelings. A lasting emotion is called an emotional state, or mood. There are many descriptions of emotional states: sadness, happiness, anger, frustration, jealousy, love, hate.

Epistemic: This has to do with knowledge (cf. ontological). Subjective knowledge relates to opinion, and objective knowledge relates to facts, observable truths.

Explicit: The term explicit is used to describe memory processes that have varying degrees of associated attention. Explicit memory processes have also been described as conscious, declarative and non-automatic.

Feelings: These are what are produced by the affective response, our response to an event that has been tagged by emotion. They largely result from hypothalamic activity.

Heuristic: A thinking shortcut, a quick way to think, which may not be completely accurate but which works most of the time. Useful when the cost of getting a decision wrong is low.

Implicit: This word is used to describe memory processes used without attention when we are conscious. Subconscious may be a better term. Implicit memory processes have also been described as unconscious, non-declarative and automatic.

Incidence: The number of new cases per population of risk in a given time period (cf. prevalence).

Instinctive Behaviour: This term has many meanings. It can be used to describe the most rapid way to act, called reflex action, or it can describe slower activity that is related to need and emotion. It has a brief mention only in this book.

Intuitive Thinking: Using our intuition or 'intuitive thinking' is thinking triggered by emotion that we then feel as affect. It often happens within milliseconds. It is different to instinctive thinking. Some authors have also included rapid thinking processes using explicit and implicit memory without affect, in the term intuitive thinking.

Knowledge: Knowledge is context-specific information learned through experience and stored using memory processes.

Learning: Learning refers to a change in behaviour resulting from acquiring knowledge about the world.

Light: Electromagnetic radiation can be produced from a variety of sources. On earth, one of the main sources is the sun, but it can also be produced from many other sources, such as electric lighting and the bioluminescence of animals like the firefly. The energy of electromagnetic radiation is transported from one location to another by waves which are fluctuations of electric and magnetic fields, hence the term electromagnetic radiation (EM radiation).

The primary properties of EM radiation are intensity, direction of movement or propagation, frequency or wavelength spectrum, and polarisation. Changes in each of these properties alter the nature of the wave. For instance, the wavelengths range from the shorter gamma rays, X-rays, through ultraviolet (UV), visible light, infrared (IR) to the longer microwaves, FM and AM and long-wave radio.

EM radiation is propagated as waves, and the energy imparted by the waves is absorbed at single locations. The way light is absorbed is similar to the way energy from moving particles is absorbed. The absorbed energy of these EM waves is called a photon, and this represents the quanta of light within the wave that can be observed by us.

'When a wave of light is transformed and absorbed as a photon, the energy of the wave instantly collapses to a single location, and this location is where the photon "arrives". This is what is called the wave function collapse. This dual wave-like and particle-like nature of light is known as the wave-particle duality' (Wikipedia, accessed 2018).

The range of EM radiation visible to us, that we call light, has a range or spectrum of wavelengths of around 400 nm for ultraviolet light, up to 700 nm for infrared light, and a range of frequencies from around 430 to 750 terahertz (THz). The speed of light in a vacuum at 299,792,458 metres per second is one of the fundamental constants of nature. It means that it takes around eight minutes and 20 seconds to travel from the sun to the earth.

This visible light is converted into neural impulses through a process called phototransduction. The conversion begins in the retina. All our visual experience relies on this neural membrane in the back of the eye. The modified output from this 'window on the world' is conveyed to the brain by one million optic nerve fibres, but nearly half of the cerebral cortex is used to process this output. Visual information that is lost in the retina 'can never be recovered'. (Kandel, 2013).

Memory: A broad range of processes that store our experience of the world. It is usually divided into short-term and long-term memory. Long-term conscious memory processes include acquisition, encoding, storage and later retrieval.

Mind: A broad term to include any neural activity within the brain.

Morpheme: The smallest unit of meaning a word can be divided into, e.g. the units 'like' and 'ly' forming the word likely.

Morphology: Morphology specifies the rules for combining words into longer words by adding prefixes and suffixes, so that, for example, the subject and predicate will agree.

MRI (Magnetic Resonance Imaging) Scan: MRI scans like PET scans are sensitive to increases in blood flow associated with increases in neural activity. However MRI requires no injection of foreign contrast material and has better spatial resolution than PET. MRI uses the magnetic properties of protons in brain tissue to obtain information about structure and function. Protons form the nucleus of the hydrogen atom and spin around the nucleus acting as small magnets, each with their own random dipole. Normally these fields are cancelled by other fields generated by other nuclei within the same tissue. But when placed in a magnetic field, these dipoles are aligned.

If a second magnetic field formed by a radiofrequency pulse is applied to the same tissue at the same time, the protons in the nucleus start to wobble instead of spinning. This is called 'precession' and creates a rotating magnetic field that changes with time, generating an electrical current which is measured by MRI. When the radio frequency pulse is turned off, the protons start to return to a lower energy state. They precess less, those that were rotating together fall out of synchrony and they revert to the alignment of the original magnetic field.

Two relaxation processes which are time dependent are measured. The slower T1-weighted image measures the righting of tipped protons as they realign with the original magnetic field, and a *higher* signal intensity is produced. The faster T2-weighted image measures the dephasing of rotating protons, and a *lower* signal intensity is produced. Protons have different relaxation rates and T1 and T2 time constants, depending on whether they are embedded in fat, grey matter, etc. The images gained are compared with calibrated MRI images.

When the brain is stimulated, several things *increase*: neural activity, blood supply to the activated region and the proportion of oxygenated blood to deoxygenated blood. MRI uses the differences in magnetic properties between oxygenated and deoxygenated blood, producing stronger signals in more active areas.

In fMRI, signals from the resting brain are compared with signals from the stimulated brain to show what areas are activated. For instance, in a condition of visual stimulation, the occipital cortex and LGN of the thalamus are activated. fMRI shows us what structures and systems of the brain are used to perform different functions, but it does not tell us how we use these areas.

Neurotransmitters: There are many different neurotransmitters. They can be roughly divided up into the small molecules and the larger peptides. There are relatively few small molecules that act as transmitters. These are produced in the cytoplasm of the cell body and travel down the axons to the nerve terminal, or they can be produced at the terminal. They can be easily taken up and released from vesicles into the synaptic space. Adrenalin is the only transmitter that is synthesised within vesicles.

Acetylcholine (ACh) is derived from dietary choline and acetyl-CoA, a common metabolite in all cells. In peripheral nervous systems, it is released by spinal motor neurons at the neuromuscular junction within muscle. In the autonomic nervous system, it is the principal neurotransmitter for all preganglionic neurons and for postganglionic neurons of the parasympathetic system. Cholinergic neurons form synapses throughout the brain. It is a principal transmitter in brain stem arousal systems.

The biogenic amines or monoamines, as a group, include the catecholamines and serotonin. Histamine has historically been included in this group, even though it is biochemically different. The catecholamines include dopamine, noradrenalin (nor-A, norepinephrine) and adrenalin (epinephrine). These are all synthesised in a common pathway from the essential amino acid tyrosine: dopamine is the precursor of noradrenalin, and noradrenalin is the precursor of adrenalin. Tyrosine is called an essential amino acid as it can't be synthesised in the body and is therefore classed as an essential element of a normal diet.

Production of these neurotransmitters is heavily regulated and varies with neuronal activity. Neurons using monoamine transmitters have similar properties that make them suitable for their role in modulation of neural activity. Many of these neurons have regular firing rates produced by internal pacemakers, making them useful in nuclei such as the basal ganglia that need to maintain a regular firing rate for muscle control.

There are four major nerve tracts within the brain that use dopamine, three arising in the midbrain. The *substantia nigra,* one of the nuclei of the basal ganglia, is important in the control of movement, and is affected in disorders like Parkinson's disease. The *mesolimbic* and *mesocortical tracts* are important in attention, emotion and affect, and motivation. Abnormalities in these tracts are involved in schizophrenia and drug addiction. Dopamine is not used in the peripheral nervous system.

Noradrenalin is used in the peripheral nervous system as a postganglionic sympathetic neurotransmitter. Within the brain, neurons with cell bodies in the locus coeruleus in the brain stem use noradrenalin as a neurotransmitter. These neurons are relatively few in number but they have diffuse, widespread connections throughout the cortex, cerebellum and spinal cord. Only a small number of neurons in the brain use adrenalin as a neurotransmitter.

Serotonin (5-Hydroxytryptamine or 5-HT) is derived from the

essential amino acid tryptophan. It is not used as a transmitter outside the brain. Within the brain it is used by neurons with cell bodies in and around the raphe nuclei of the brain stem that have diffuse, widespread connections throughout the brain and spinal cord.

Histamine is derived from the essential amino acid histidine. As a neurotransmitter, it is concentrated in the hypothalamus regulating hormone secretion. It has widespread effects outside the nervous system. It is released by mast cells in inflammation and is responsible for the itch in allergy. It controls the secretion of acid in the stomach and affects blood vessels and other smooth muscle.

Amino acid transmitters such as glutamate and GABA (γ-aminobutyric acid), are non-essential amino acids and able to be synthesised within neurones. Glutamate is the neurotransmitter commonly used at excitatory synapses throughout the central nervous system. Conversely, GABA is a major neurotransmitter in inhibitory neurons and interneurons and is present in high concentrations throughout the central nervous system. The excitatory effects of alcohol are partly due to GABA inhibition.

The larger short peptides that act as neurotransmitters are produced in the endoplasmic reticulum and the Golgi apparatus within the cell and are transported by fast axonal transport within vesicles to the nerve end. There are more than 50 short neuroactive peptides, and they can be grouped into less than 10 families depending on their structure or the genes that encode them.

Some of these transmitters act on targets outside the brain, such as angiotensin acting on the kidney, and some are products of neuroendocrine secretion, such as oxytocin. These can act as hormones in some tissues, or as neurotransmitters when released close to a neuron, causing excitation or inhibition or both.

Some neuroactive peptides modulate sensory perception and emotion within the brain. Substance P and the encephalins are implicated in the perception of pain. Others are involved in the complicated reactions to stress, such as the adrenocorticotropic hormone (ACTH) that increases production of cortisol in the adrenal cortex.

Ontological: This refers to anything concerned with existence (cf. epistemological). This includes entities whose existence is ontologically objective, e.g. mountains and the tectonic plates of the earth's crust that everyone can see and experience. Entities whose existence is ontologically subjective are experienced internally and include feelings such as pain or itch. We can feel them ourselves, but no one else can. Consciousness and our internal narrative are ontologically subjective.

Perception: We are bombarded by sensory stimuli every moment of every day for the whole of our lives. Perception is how we accept, modify then use the neural activity these sensory stimuli create to produce a percept, an interpretation. It can be unconscious or conscious. It relates to 'reality' and the related questions: what is the true nature of reality and do we all perceive reality in the same way? Do you see what I see?

PET (Positron Emission Tomography) Scan: To produce a PET image of the brain, the patient is injected with a dose of a radiopharmaceutical (a radioactive compound). This is a substance that can be absorbed and concentrated by certain groups of cells in the brain. For example, fluorodeoxyglucose (FDG) is glucose attached to an isotope of fluoride produced in a cyclotron after being bombarded by protons. The cells in the brain which are more active in a given period of time after the injection will absorb more FDG, because they have a higher metabolism and need more energy and a higher blood flow.

The fluoride atom in the FDG molecule decays emitting a positron. When a positron collides with a nearby electron, two beams of gamma rays moving in opposite directions will be produced. The energy from this will be picked up by crystal detectors placed in a ring around the patient, producing small pulses of light which are then amplified and analysed by computer and shown as an image on the PET scanner. The whole process is called scintigraphy. Because the site of annihilation of the positron is often some millimetres away from where it was released, the resolution of PET images is limited to between three and eight millimetres.

The computer shows an image which is like a section, or a slice, across the brain. The slice can follow a horizontal orientation (called transverse section) or a vertical orientation (called a coronal section). The intensity of activity can be shown in shades of grey, where black means no activity and pure white the highest count level. Or the same image can be displayed in false colour, where each level of grey is converted into a shade of colour, red indicating the highest activity count, then yellow, green, blue, violet and black.

Specific activities in the brain can be measured by using radiopharmaceuticals that attach themselves to certain neurons. For example, a radiopharmaceutical which has a strong affinity for cells containing the neurotransmitter dopamine, concentrates in an area of the brain called the basal nuclei which are responsible for the control of movement. These cells are damaged in Parkinson's disease, so they have a lower concentration of dopamine. PET is an excellent method to quantify the brain function in people with this disease.

Phoneme: Any unit of sound that distinguishes between words, e.g. in English the sounds /r/ and /l/ that differentiate between rock and lock.

Phonetic: Relating to the sounds of speech.

Phonology: This specifies the rules for combining sound elements and phonemes into words. The sound elements do not have meaning in themselves, e.g. D-O-G has a different meaning to G-O-D.

Prevalence: The number of cases existing within a defined population at risk at any given time (cf. incidence).

Probability: Probability is the likelihood of an event happening, and the percentage chance of an event happening within a sample space, expressed as a number between zero and one. We use phrases such as 'there's a probability of 0.7 that event A will happen, given certain conditions'. We can also use the term 'risk' when we talk about probabilities and we use percentages when describing it — we say 'there is a 70% risk of event A happening given certain conditions'.

Conditional probability can be defined as 'the likelihood that something is true, given a piece of information' — if event A happens, what is the likelihood that event B will happen? It is all about interpreting what we see, realising that the information is limited and trying to find the truth or predict the future. What can I infer from this information? What is the likelihood that what I see before me really does mean that this or that is going to happen? What is this person really like, based on what I can see? We try and evaluate the probability of uncertain events happening so we can make decisions about what to do.

Note that this is not the prior probability (the prevalence of the disease in the practice population) but the conditional probability (the probability of the disease, given a patient's symptoms). A synonym for *conditional probability* is *predictive value*: the predictive value of a symptom for a disease. Predictive value varies with prevalence.

The original theorem describing conditional probability is Bayes' theorem. Thomas Bayes (c.1702–17 April 1761) was a British mathematician and Presbyterian minister, known for having formulated a specific case of the theorem that bears his name and which was published posthumously. It is an equation about conditional probability where the probability of an event occurring is conditional on the probability of another related event. In medicine it is used in situations where we want to know what the probability of diagnosis is when, say, we receive a test result. If we label the test result as event A, we estimate the probability that an event B, such as the diagnosis, has occurred, based on the result of the test. We can then judge what we think the patient has, and can decide to start treatment or seek more evidence.

One of the ways of stating the formula is:

$$P(B \backslash A) = P(B \cap A) \ / \ P(A)$$

This translates into: the probability that event B will occur given that event A, the test result, has occurred (in other words, the percentage chance that a result means whether you have the disease or not, the predictive value or the post-test probability), is equal to the numbers of true positives (related to the numbers of people that truly have the disease if they have a positive result, or the sensitivity of a test), divided by the natural frequency of event A happening, termed the prevalence.

Bayes' theorem can be used to calculate post-test probabilities (or odds) based on pretest probabilities and the sensitivity and specificity of a test. Sensitivity is a measure of how many people with the problem will test positive and specificity is a measure of how many people who test negative won't have the disorder. All are measures of how effective a symptom or sign or test is in identifying a disease and in discriminating between it and other diseases or an otherwise normal state of health.

Sensitivities and specificities are not constants for a particular event. They are context specific. Consider the example of urine testing for pregnancy. It is not until two to three weeks after conception, or four to five weeks after the last period that most urine tests become positive in a normal pregnancy. The test has different sensitivity and specificity depending on the gestation and health of the pregnancy.

The important thing to realise is that probabilities give you guesstimates only about what a piece of information means.. Few examples come near a probability of one or zero. Probability can be actual (objective) or perceived (subjective). Objective probability is produced by external measurement. Perceived probability is measured internally and is similar to cue weighting as discussed in the chapter on perception.

Prosody: The pattern of intonation and stress in words which, for example, allow us to distinguish questions from statements.

Reflex Action: Reflex action describes the rapid action produced in response to a strong stimulus using minimal brain activity.

Response: This word is classically used by behaviourists to explain any behaviour related to a stimulus. It is similar in meaning to reaction.

Rostral: This means 'towards the head'. Because the direction of the brain circuits changes by 90 degrees at the brain stem, in the brain, rostral often means 'in front of' not above (cf. caudal).

Satisfycing: A neat term coined by Herbert A Simon in 1956 — a combination of satisfy and suffice. It was a decision-making heuristic where a search was made of all the available alternatives until an acceptable threshold was reached. The term was used as part of the concept of bounded rationality, in contrast to the concepts of rational choice theory which had come to be seen as unrealistic.

Stimulus: This word was used by the behaviourists, including B F Skinner, to describe how human behaviour can arise after presentation of a simple stimulus such as light. Classically, stimuli have been classified as 'sensory', 'perceptual', 'semantic' or 'conceptual', and 'external' when coming from the outside, or 'internal' when they have been produced using memory and emotion. They can be described as weak or strong. Often the word 'cue' is used to describe information we use in thinking and acting. 'Sensory stimuli' are small packages of information we can use to respond quickly and are similar to information in cues.

Syntax: This specifies how words are to be combined into phrases and sentences so the meaning will be clear.

Thinking: Classically related to contemplation. Similar to reasoning and rational thought, thinking usually means conscious, attentive activity mediated by the frontal cortex and using the full range of our memory, perception and emotional abilities. Thinking can also be used as a generic term for brain activity when we are awake. It can mean many things to many different people.

Unconscious: Relative absence of wakefulness or alertness or arousal. The level of consciousness can be graded using assessments of the state of arousal, and motor and verbal responses using the Glasgow Coma Scale.

Bibliography

Alem, Sylvain et al (2016). 'Associative mechanisms allow for social learning and cultural transmission of string pulling in an insect.' *PLOS Biology*, 4 October 2016

Allman, Melissa J, Teki, Sundeep, Griffiths, Timothy D, and Meck, Warren H (2014). 'Properties of the internal clock: first- and second-order principles of subjective time.' *Annual Review of Psychology*, **65**: 743–771

Appleyard, Bryan (2011). The Brain is Wider than the Sky — Why Simple Solutions Don't work in a complex world. London: Weidenfeld and Nicolson

Ashton-James, Claire E, Richardson, Daniel C, Williams, Amanda C de C, Bianchi-Berthouze, Nadia, and Dekker, Peter H (2014). 'Impact of pain behaviors on evaluations of warmth and competence.' *Pain*, **155**: Issue 12; 2439–2724 (December 2014)

Baron, Jonathan (2008). *Thinking and Deciding, Fourth Edition.* Cambridge: Cambridge University Press

Barrett, Lisa F, Mesquita, Batja, Ochsner, Kevin N, Gross, James J

(2007). 'The experience of emotion.' *Annual Review of Psychology*, **58**: 373–403

Bell, Vaughan (2013). 'Dopamine may be the media's neurotransmitter of choice for scare stories about addiction, but the reality is far more nuanced.' *Guardian Weekly*, 15 February 2013

Bernstein, Carl (1992). 'The idiot culture — Reflections of post-Watergate journalism.' The *New Republic*, 8 June 1992 pp. 22–28

Brodmann, Karl (1909). Vergleichende Lokalisationslehre der Großhirnrinde in ihren Prinzipien dargestellt auf Grund des Zellenbaues. Leipzig: Barth, 1909

Brunswik, E (1952). The conceptual framework of psychology. *International Encyclopaedia of Unified Sciences*, **1**: No. 10. Chicago: University of Chicago Press

Brunswik, E (1955). 'Representative design and probabilistic theory in a functional psychology.' *Psychological Review*, **62**: 193–217

Brunswik, E (1956). *Perception and the Representative Design of Psychological Experiments*, (2nd ed.). Berkeley, CA, US: University of California Press

Budson, Andrew E, and Price, Bruce H (2005). 'Memory dysfunction.' *The New England Journal of Medicine*, **352**: 692–699

Burkeman, Oliver (2014). 'This column will change your life: random decisions.' www.theguardian.com 10 October 2014

Burkeman, Oliver (2015). 'What is an emotion?' www.theguardian.com 14 August 2015

Carlén, Marie (2017). 'What constitutes the prefrontal cortex?' *Science*, **358**: 478–482. 27 October 2017

Collins, Darron (2017). 'Hard data and human empathy.' *Science*, **358**: 142. 6 Oct 2017

Connolly, Terry, Arkes, Hal R, and Hammond, Kenneth R (Eds) (2000). *Judgment and Decision Making — An Interdisciplinary Reader*. Cambridge, UK: Cambridge University Press

Conway, Bevil R, Rehding, Alexander (2013). 'Neuroaesthetics and the trouble with beauty.' *PLOS Biology*, Vol. **11**: issue 3/e1001504. March 2013. www.plosbiology.org

Correa, Kelly A, Stone, Bradly T, Stikic, Maja, Johnson, Robin R, and Berka, Chris (2015). 'Characterizing donation behavior from psychophysiological indices of narrative experience.' *Front Neurosci*, **9**: 301. 31 Aug 2015

Damasio, A R (1994). Descartes' Error — Emotion, Reason and the Human Brain. New York: Putnam

Damasio, A R (1999). The Feeling of What Happens — Body and Emotion in the Making of Consciousness. Harcourt Brace, 1999

Darwin, Charles (1965). *The Expressions of the Emotions in Man and Animal*. Chicago: University of Chicago Press. (The original work was published in 1872)

Daston, L (1998). *Classical Probability in the Enlightenment*. NJ: Princeton University Press

Decety, Jean, Bartal, Ben-Ami, Uzefovsky, Florina and Knafo-Noam, Ariel (2015). 'Empathy as a driver of prosocial behaviour: highly conserved neurobehavioural mechanisms across species.' *Philo-*

sophical Transactions of the Royal Society — Biological Sciences, 7 December 2015

Dehaene, Stanislas, Lau, Hakwan and Kouider, Sid (2017). 'What is consciousness, and could machines have it?' *Science,* **358**: 486–492. 27 Oct 2017

Dietrich, Arne (2004). 'The cognitive neuroscience of creativity.' *Psychonomic Bulletin & Review,* **11**: 6; 1011–26

Dietrich, Arne and Kanso, Riam (2010). 'A review of EEG, ERP, and neuroimaging studies of creativity and insight.' *Psychological Bulletin,* **136**: No. 5; 822–848

Dowie, Jack and Elstein, Arthur (Eds) (1988). *Professional Judgment. A Reader in Clinical Decision Making.* NY: Cambridge University Press

Draguhn, Andreas (2018). 'Making room for new memories.' *Science,* **359**: 1461–62. 30 March 2018

Dreyfus, H L and Dreyfus, S E (1986). Mind Over Machine — The Power of Human Intuition and Expertise in the Era of the Computer. NY: The Free Press

Durrett, Richard (1994). *The Essentials of Probability.* Belmont, CA: Duxbury Press

Edelman, G M (2004). *Wider Than the Sky — The Phenomenal Gift of Consciousness.* New Haven, CT: Yale University Press

Edwards, W (1954). 'The theory of decision making.' *Psychological Bulletin,* **51**: 4; 380–417

Ekman, Paul (1999). 'Basic Emotions.' Ch. 3 in *Handbook of Cognition and*

Emotion, Eds: Dalgleish, T and Power, M. John Wiley and Sons. https://onlinelibrary.wiley.com/doi/abs/10.1002/0470013494.ch3

Elliot, Andrew J and Maier, Markus A (2014). 'Color psychology: Effects of perceiving color on psychological functioning in humans.' *Annual Review of Psychology*, **65**: 95–120

Elstein, Arthur S and Bordage, Georges (1998). 'Psychology of Clinical Reasoning.' In: *Professional Judgement: A Reader in Clinical Decision Making*, Eds: Dowie, Jack and Elstein, Arthur. Cambridge, UK: Cambridge University Press

Elstein, Arthur S, Kagan, Norman, Shulman, Lee S, Jason, Hillard and Loupe, Michael J (1972). 'Methods and theory in the study of medical inquiry.' *Journal of Medical Education*, **47**: 85–92

Elstein, Arthur S, Shulman, Lee S and Sprafka, Sarah A et al (1978). *Medical Problem Solving — An Analysis of Clinical Reasoning.* Cambridge, MA: Harvard University Press

Felix-Ortiz, Ada C, Beyeler, Anna, Seo, Changwoo, Leppla, Christopher A, Wildes, Craig P, Tye, K M (2013). 'BLA to vHPC inputs modulate anxiety-related behaviors.' *Neuron*, **78**: 658–664. 21 August 2013

Fielder, Klaus and Juslin, Peter (2006). 'Taking the interface between mind and environment seriously.' In: *Information Sampling and Adaptive Cognition*, Part 1: Introduction. NY: Cambridge University Press

Fields, Howard L (2014). 'More pain; less gain.' *Science*, **345**: 513–14. 1 August 2014

Finucane, M L, Alhakami, A, Slovic, P, Johnson, S M (2000). 'The affect heuristic in judgments of risks and benefits.' *Journal of Behavioral Decision Making*, **13**: 1–17

Fox, Craig R and Tversky, Amos (1998). 'A belief-based account of decision under uncertainty.' *Management Science*, **44**: No. 7; July 1998

Frankland, Paul W and Josselyn, Sheena A (2018). 'Facing your fears.' *Science*, **360**: 1186–87. 15 June 2018

Freedland, Jonathan (2017). 'British voters look like they're rejecting Santa and embracing Scrooge. Why?' www.guardian.com/opinion, 19 May 2017

Gehring, William J and Willoughby, Adrian R (2002). 'The medial frontal cortex and the rapid processing of monetary gains and losses.' *Science*, **295**: issue 5563, 2279–82

Gentner, Dedre and Stevens, Albert L (Eds) (1983). *Mental Models.* NJ: Lawrence Erlbaum Associates

Gigerenzer, Gerd and Goldstein, Daniel G (1996). Reasoning the fast and frugal way: models of bounded rationality.' *Psychological Review*, **103**: 4; 650–69

Gigerenzer, Gerd and Brighton, Henry (2009). 'Homo heuristicus: why biased minds make better inferences.' *Topics in Cognitive Science*, **1**: 107–143

Gilovich, Thomas and Griffin, Dale (2002). 'Introduction — Heuristics and biases: then and now.' In: *Heuristics and Biases — The Psychology of Intuitive Judgment*, Eds: Gilovich, Thomas, Griffin, Dale and Kahneman, Daniel. Cambridge: Cambridge University Press

Gladwell, Malcolm (2005). *Blink — The Power of Thinking Without Thinking*. London: Penguin

Gleitman, Henry, Fridlund, Alan J, and Reisberg, Daniel (2004). *Psychology*. NY: W W Norton and Company

Goethe, Johann Wolfgang von (1777). *The Sorrows of Young Werther.* In First Signet Classics, published 2013. UK: Penguin

Goldstein, William M, and Hogarth, Robin M (1997). *Research on Judgment and Decision Making — Currents, Connections, and Controversies.* Cambridge: Cambridge University Press

Grossberg, Stephen and Pearson, Lance R (2008). 'Laminar cortical dynamics of cognitive and motor working memory, sequence learning and performance: toward a unified theory of how the cerebral cortex works.' *Psychological Review,* **115**: 3; 677–732

Hamm, Robert M (1988). 'Clinical intuition and clinical analysis: expertise and the cognitive continuum.' In: *Professional Judgment — A Reader in Clinical Decision Making,* Eds: Dowie, Jack and Elstein, Arthur S. Cambridge, UK: Cambridge University Press

Hammond, Kenneth R (1978). 'Toward increasing competence of thought in public policy formation.' In: *Judgment and Decision in Public Policy Formation,* Ed: Hammond, K R pp. 11–32. Boulder, CO: Westview Press

Harari, Yuval Noah (2011). *Sapiens: A Brief History of Humankind.* London: Vintage Books

Harlow, John Martyn (1868). *Recovery from the passage of an iron bar through the head.* Publications of The Massachusetts Medical Society, **2**: 3; 327–47. For a link to download a PDF: https://collections.nlm.nih.gov/catalog/nlm:nlmuid-66210360R-bk

Hawking, Stephen W (1988). *A Brief History of Time.* NY: Bantam

Hebb, D O (1949). *The Organization of Behavior — A Neuropsychological Theory.* NY: Wiley

Henley, Jon (2009). 'The truth about lying.' www.theguardian.com 12 May 2009. Accessed 28 August 2017

Hölzel, Britta K et al (2010). 'Stress reduction correlates with structural changes in the amygdala.' *Social Cognitive and Affective Neuroscience,* **5**: Issue 1; 11–17

Hosoda, M, Stone-Romero, E F, and Coats, G (2003). 'The effects of physical attractiveness on job-related outcomes: a meta-analysis of experimental studies.' *Personnel Psychology,* **56**: 2; 431–462

James, William (1884). 'What is an emotion?' *Mind,* **9**: 34; 188–205

Kahneman, Daniel (2011). *Thinking, fast and slow.* London: Penguin Group

Kahneman, Daniel and Tversky, Amos (1973). 'On the psychology of prediction.' *Psychological Review,* **80**: 4; 237–251

Kahneman, Daniel and Tversky, Amos (1984). 'Choices, values, and frames.' *American Psychologist,* **39**: 4; 341–350. Also in: *Choices, Values and Frames,* Eds: Kahneman, Daniel and Tversky, Amos.(2000) NY: Cambridge University Press

Kahneman, Daniel and Tversky, Amos (1996). 'Theoretical notes on the reality of cognitive illusions.' *Psychological Review,* **103**: 3; 582–591

Kandel, Eric R, Schwartz, James H, Jessell, Thomas M, Siegelbaum, Steven A, Hudspeth, A J (Eds) (2013). *Principles of Neural Science, Fifth Edition.* USA: McGraw-Hill

Kaptchuk, Ted J and Miller, Franklin G (2015). 'Placebo effects in medicine.' *The New England Journal of Medicine,* **373**: 1; 8–9

Karelaia, Natalia and Hogarth, Robin M (2008). 'Determinants of linear judgment: a meta-analysis of lens model studies.' *Psychological Bulletin*, **134**: 3; 404–426

Kerouac, Jack (1958). *The Dharma Bums*. US: Penguin 1976

Khodagholy, Dion, Gelinas, Jennifer N and Buzsáki, György (2017). 'Learning-enhanced coupling between ripple oscillations in association cortices and hippocampus.' *Science*, **358**: 369–372. 20 October 2017

Koch, Christof (2014). 'Neuronal "superhub" might generate consciousness.' *Scientific American*. 1 November 2014

Koestler, Arthur (1967). *The Ghost in the Machine*. England: Arkana Books

Krishnamurthy, Kamesh, Nassar, Matthew R, Sarode, Shilpa and Gold, Joshua I (2017). 'Arousal- related adjustments of perceptual biases optimize perception in dynamic environments.' *Nature Human Behaviour*, 8 May 2017. www.nature.com/articles

Landi, Sofia M and Freiwald, Winrich A (2017). 'Two areas for familiar face recognition in the primate brain.' *Science*, **357**: 592–595. 11 August 2017

Langford, Dale J et al (2006). 'Social modulation of pain as evidence for empathy in mice.' *Science*, **312**: 1967–1970. 30 June 2006

Lavie, Nilli (2010). 'Attention, distraction and cognitive control under load.' *Current Directions in Psychological Science*, **19**: 143–148

Le Van Quyen, Michel and Rudrauf, David (2015). 'Top-down causation in biological systems: foundations and applications.' Research Topic in *Journal of Cognitive Neuroscience*. http://journal.frontiersin.org/journal/neuroscience. Accessed 20 September 2015

Lee, Sunyoung, Pitesa, Marko, Pillutla, Madan M and Thau, Stefan (2015). 'When beauty helps and when it hurts: an organizational context model of attractiveness discrimination in selection decisions.' *Organizational Behavior and Human Decision Processes*, **128**: 15–28.

Leroy, Sophie (2009). 'Why is it so hard to do my work? The challenge of attention residue when switching between work tasks.' *Organizational Behavior and Human Decision Processes*, **109**: Issue 2; 168–181. July 2009

Lesburguères, Edith, Gobbo, Olevero L, Alaux-Cantin, Stéphanie, Hambucken, Anne, Trifilieff, Pierre and Bontempi, Bruno (2011). 'Early tagging of cortical networks is required for the formation of enduring associative memory.' *Science*, **31**: 924–928. 18 February 2011

Levitin, Daniel J (2006). *This is Your Brain on Music — The Science of a Human Obsession*. NY: Plume

Lhermitte, F (1983). '"Utilization behaviour" and its relation to lesions of the frontal lobes.' *Brain*, **106**: 237–255

Lhermitte, F, Pillon, B, and Serdaru, M (1986). 'Human autonomy and the frontal lobes: Part 1. Imitation and utilization behavior: A neuropsychological study of 75 patients.' *Annals of Neurology*, **19**: 326–334

Libet, B, Gleason, C A, Wright, E W and Pearl, D K (1983). 'Time of conscious intention to act in relation to onset of cerebral activity (readiness-potential): the unconscious initiation of a freely voluntary act.' *Brain*, **106**: 623–642

Loewenstein, George F, Weber, Elke U, Hsee, Christopher K and

Welch, Ned (2001). 'Risk as feelings.' *Psychological Bulletin*, **127**: No. 2; 267–286

Ma, Qingguo, Hu, Yue, Jiang, Shushu and Meng, Liang (2016). 'The undermining effect of facial attractiveness on brain responses to fairness in the Ultimatum Game: an ERP study.' *Frontiers in Neuroscience*, **9**: article 77. 10 Mar 2016. www.frontiersin.org

Margoliash, D and Tchernichovski, O (2015). 'Marmoset kids actually listen.' *Science*, **349**: issue 6249; 688–689

Maril, Anat, Wagner, A D and Schacter, Daniel L (2001). 'On the tip of the tongue: an event-related fMRI study of semantic retrieval failure and cognitive conflict.' *Neuron*, **31**: 653–660

Markman, Arthur B and Gentner, Dedre (2001). 'Thinking.' *Annual Review Psychology*, **52**: 223–247

Martynoga, Ben (2018). 'What does running do to your brain?' www.theguardian.com 21 June 2018. Accessed 22 June 2018

Maslow, A H (1943). 'A theory of human motivation.' *Psychological Review*, **50:** 4; 370–396

McWhinney, Ian R (1989). *A Textbook of Family Medicine*. Oxford: Oxford University Press

Meehl, Paul E (1954). *Clinical Versus Statistical Prediction — A Theoretical Analysis and a Review of the Evidence*. Minneapolis: University of Minnesota Press

Mendl, Michael T and Paul, Elizabeth S (2016). 'Bee happy: bumblebees show decision-making that reflects emotion-like states.' *Science*, **353**: 1499. 30 September 2016

Miller, George (2000). 'General Introduction.' p. 3 in *Judgment and Decision Making — An Interdisciplinary Reader.* (2nd ed.), Eds: Connolly, Terry, Arkes, Hal R, Hammond, Kenneth R. Cambridge: Cambridge University Press

Mortenson, Greg and Relin, D O (2007). *Three Cups of Tea: One Man's Mission to Promote Peace ... One School at a Time.* United Kingdom: Penguin Books

Mullis, Kary B (1990). 'The unusual origin of the polymerase chain reaction.' *Scientific American,* **262**: No. 4; 36–43

Nagel, T (1993). 'What is the Mind-Body Problem?' In: *Experimental and Theoretical Studies of Consciousness (Ciba Foundation Symposium 174),* Eds: Block, G R and Marsh, J. Chichester, UK: John Wiley

Namburi, Praneeth et al (2016). 'A circuit mechanism for differentiating positive and negative associations.' *Nature,* **520**: 675–678

Norimoto, Hiroaki et al (2018). 'Hippocampal ripples down-regulate synapses.' *Science,* **359**: 1524–1527. 30 March 2018

Oakley, David A and Halligan, Peter W (2017). 'Chasing the rainbow: the non-conscious nature of being.' *Frontiers in Psychology,* **8**: article 1924. November 2017. Accessed at www.frontiersin.org

Pinker, Steven (2018). 'The media exaggerates negative news. This distortion has consequences.' www.theguardian.com 17 Feb 2018. Accessed 3 Mar 2018

Powers, A R, Mathys, C and Corlett, P R (2017). 'Pavlovian conditioning-induced hallucinations result from overweighting of perceptual priors.' *Science,* **357**: issue 6351; 596–600

Pressey, Sidney L, Robinson, Francis P and Horrocks, John E (1959). *Psychology in Education*. NY: Harper and Brothers

Pryor, Francis (2003). *Britain BC — Life in Britain and Ireland before the Romans*. London: Harper Perennial

Rajan, Kanaka, Harvey, Christopher D and Tank, David W (2016). 'Recurrent network models of sequence generation and memory.' *Neuron*, **90**: issue 1; 128–142. 8 August 2016

Ramirez, Steve (2017). 'Crystallizing a memory.' *Science*, **360**: 1182–83. 15 June 2018

Reardon, Sara (2017). 'A giant neuron found wrapped around entire mouse brain.' *Nature*, **543**: 14–15. 2 Mar 2017

Reber, Rolf, Winkielman, Piotr, and Schwarz, Norbert (1998). 'Effects of perceptual fluency on affective judgments.' *Psychological Science*, **9**: 45–48

Ridderinkhof, K Richard, Ullsperger, Markus, Crone, Eveline A and Nieuwenhuis, Sander (2004). 'The role of the medial frontal cortex in cognitive control.' *Science*, **306**: 5695; 443–447

Robbins, Tom (1984). *Jitterbug Perfume*. US: Bantam

Rowe, James B, Toni, Ivan, Josephs, Oliver, Frackowiak, Richard S J, Passingham, Richard E (2000). 'The prefrontal cortex: response selection or maintenance within working memory?' *Science*, **282**: 1656–1662. 2 Jun 2000

Sartre, Jean-Paul (1938). *Nausea*. Australia: Penguin (2010)

Sartre, Jean-Paul (1945). 'Existentialism and humanism.' Lecture at the Club Maintenant, Paris, France, October 1945. Reproduced in:

Jean-Paul Sartre — Basic Writings, Ed: Priest, Stephen. London: Routledge, 2001

Savage, Leonard J (1954). *The Foundations of Statistics.* NY: Wiley

Schacter, Daniel L (2001). *The Seven Sins of Memory — How the Mind Forgets and Remembers.* Boston: Houghton Mifflin

Schwarz, Norbert (2002). 'Feelings as information: moods influence judgments and processing strategies.' In: *Heuristics and Biases: The Psychology of Intuitive Judgment,* Eds: Gilovich, Thomas, Griffin, Dale and Kahneman, Daniel. pp. 534–547. NY: Cambridge University Press

Searle, John R (1998). 'How to study consciousness scientifically.' In: *Towards an Understanding of Integrative Brain Functions,* Eds: Fuxe, K, Grillner, S, Hökfelt, T, Olson, L and Agnati, L F. pp. 379–387. Amsterdam: Elsevier

Searle, John R (2013). 'Theory of mind and Darwin's legacy.' 18 June 2013 supplement at http://www.pnas.org/content/110/Supplement_2/10343

Siclari, Francesca et al (2017). 'The neural correlates of dreaming.' *Nature Neuroscience,* 10 April 2017. www.nature.com

Simon, Herbert A (1947). *Administrative Behavior.* NY: The Macmillan Company

Simon, Herbert A (1955). 'A behavioral model of rational choice.' *The Quarterly Journal of Economics,* **69**: 99–118

Simon, Herbert A (1956). 'Rational choice and the structure of the environment.' *Psychological Review,* **63:** 2; 129–138

Slovic, Paul, Finucane, Melissa L, Peters, Ellen and MacGregor, Donald G (2004). 'Risk as analysis and risk as feelings: some thoughts about affect, reason, risk, and rationality.' *Risk Analysis,* **24**: 2; 311–32

Solé, Ricard and Goodwin, Brian (2000). *Signs of Life — How Complexity Pervades Biology.* NY: Basic Books

Solzhenitsyn, Alexander Isayevich (1969). *Cancer Ward.* Translated by Nicholas Bethell and David Burg. UK: Penguin

Szegedi et al (2016). 'Plasticity in single axon glutamatergic connection to GABAergic interneurons regulates complex events in the human neocortex.' *PLOS Biology.* 9 November 2016

Taleb, Nassim Nicholas (2012). *Antifragile — How to Live in a World We Don't Understand.* Melbourne, Australia: Penguin Group

Thaler, Richard H and Sunstein, Cass R (2009). *Nudge — Improving decisions about health, wealth and happiness.* Australia: Penguin Group

Thorndike, Edward L (1920). 'A constant error in psychological ratings.' *Journal of Applied Psychology,* **4**: 1; 25–29

Todorov, Alexander, Pakrashi, Manish and Oosterhof, Nikolaas N (2009). 'Evaluating faces on trustworthiness after minimal time exposure.' *Social Cognition,* **27**: 813–33

Turing, Alan M (1953). 'The chemical basis of morphogenesis.' *Philosophical Transactions of the Royal Society (Series B),* **237**: 641; 37–72

Tversky, Amos and Kahneman, Daniel (1974). 'Judgment under uncertainty: heuristics and biases.' *Science,* **185**: 1124–1131

Tversky, Amos and Kahneman, Daniel (1983). 'Extensional versus intuitive reasoning: the conjunction fallacy in probability judgment.' *Psychological Review*, **91**: 293–315

Tversky, Amos and Kahneman, Daniel (1992). 'Advances in prospect theory: cumulative representation of uncertainty.' *Journal of Risk and Uncertainty*, **5**: 297–323

Tversky, Amos, Koehler, Derek J (1994). 'Support theory: a non-extensional representation of subjective probability.' *Psychological Review*, **101**: 4; 547–567

Underwood, Emily (2016). 'How the body learns to hurt.' *Science*, **354**: 694. 11 November 2016

Van Laer, T, de Ruyter, K D, Visconti, L M and Wetzels, M (2012). 'The extended transportation-imagery model: a meta-analysis of the antecedents and consequences of consumers' narrative transportation.' *Journal of Consumer Research*, **40**: 797–817

Varèse, Edgard and Chou, Wen-chung (1966). 'The liberation of sound.' *Perspectives of New Music*, **5**: No. 1 (Autumn–Winter); 11–19

von Neumann, John and Morgenstern, Oskar (1944, 1947, 1953) *Theory of Games and Economic Behavior*. (Three editions). Princeton: Princeton University Press

Wager, Tor D et al (2013). 'An fMRI-based neurologic signature of physical pain.' *The New England Journal of Medicine*, **368**: 1388–97

Wegner, Daniel M (2003). *The Illusion of Conscious Will*. Cambridge, MA: Bradford Books

Webb, Richard (2016). 'Is time an illusion?' *New Scientist*, 3 September 2016, p. 37

Weiner, Jonathan (2006). 'Darwin at the Zoo.' *Scientific American*, 1 Dec 2006

Wilber, Ken (1995). *Sex, Ecology and Spirituality — The Spirit of Evolution.* NY: Shambhala

Wilde, Oscar (1891). *The Picture of Dorian Gray*. Australia: Penguin Classics edition (2008), edited with an introduction and notes by Robert Mighall.

Winston, Robert (2002). *Human Instinct — How Our Primeval Impulses Shape Our Modern Lives*. London: Bantam Press

Won Bang, Ji, Shibata, Kazuhisa, Frank, Sebastian M, Walsh, Edward G, Greenlee, Mark W, Watanabe, Takeo and Sasaki, Yuka (2018). 'Consolidation and reconsolidation share behavioural and neurochemical mechanisms.' *Nature Human Behaviour*, **2**: 507–13. July 2018

Zhu, N, Cai, Y H, Sun, F W, Yang-yang, Y F (2015). 'Mapping the emotional landscape: the role of specific emotions in conceptual categorization.' *Acta Psychol, (Amst.)* **159**: 41–51

Zhu, Xueling et al (2017). 'Rumination and default mode network subsystems connectivity in first-episode, drug-naive young patients with major depressive disorder.' www.nature.com/scientificreports. 22 Feb 2017. Accessed 23 Jun 2018

Zovkic, Iva B, Guzman-Karlsson, Mikael C and Sweatt, J David (2013). 'Epigenetic regulation of memory formation and maintenance.' *Learning & Memory*, **20:** 2; 61–74. February 2013. http://learnmem.cshlp.org/content/20/2/61.full

Miscellaneous References

Thompson, Luke (2017). From Tauranga, New Zealand, interviewed on the Saturday morning radio programme on RNZ National, 21 January 2017

http://www.philipgoffphilosophy.com Accessed 14 October 2018

http://www.philpapers.org Accessed 22 October 2018

http://www.unisaustralia.com/university-quizzes-problems-brain-teasers-and-experiments/psychologicall-illusions-and-puzzles/cognitive-psychological-optical-illusions/ Accessed 7 May 2017

http://www.wikipedia.org/wiki/light Accessed 6 March 2018

http://www.wikipedia.org/hippocampus Accessed 4 August 2018

http://wikipedia.org/Phineasgage Accessed 7 December 2017

https://en.wikipedia.org/wiki/Priming_(psychology) Accessed December 2017

http://www.pnas.org/content/110/Supplement_2/10343. 'Theory of Mind and Darwin's Legacy' by John Searle in the 18 June 2013 supplement.

About the Author

Dr Graham Desborough has been a General Practitioner since 1982. In 1994, he wrote a Masters dissertation on judgement and decision making. He then set out to explain how we think. Finally, this is the result. His other main interests are mountaineering, photography and his family that now includes three daughters and four grandchildren. He currently lives in Auckland, New Zealand.

www.drgrahamdesborough.com

Acknowledgements

There are so many people that have given their support to me while writing this book: my parents John and Moira Desborough, my brother Ken Desborough, my sister Sue Miller, my three daughters Annabel Quinn, Charlotte Henderson, Sarah-Jane Nicholson; members of the Wednesday night club Terry Clark, Patrick Chandulal, Duane Eagle, Mark Griffen, Andrew Horton, John McCarthy, David Montgomery, Neal Murphy, Kevin Smith and Richard Stevens; my editors Geoff Walker, Adrienne Charlton and Eva Chan; my publisher Martin Taylor from Digital Strategies; and members of the NZSA (Pen) Auckland Branch, in particular Brent Leslie and Thomas Ryan. There have been numerous others in bars and in mountain huts who have given me the energy to complete this task. I thank you all.

www.ingramcontent.com/pod-product-compliance
Ingram Content Group UK Ltd.
Pitfield, Milton Keynes, MK11 3LW, UK
UKHW020131250726
13967UKWH00002B/593

9 780473 467081